The McNeills' SR Ranch

NUMBER TWENTY-EIGHT
The Centennial Series
of the Association of Former Students,
Texas A&M University

The McNeills' SR Ranch

100 YEARS IN BLANCO CANYON

By J. C. ("Cap") McNeill III

FOREWORD BY DAVID J. MURRAH

TEXAS A&M UNIVERSITY PRESS : COLLEGE STATION

The paper used in this book meets the minimum requirements
of the American National Standard for Permanence
of Paper for Printed Library Materials, Z39.48-1984.
Binding materials have been chosen for durability.

Library of Congress Cataloging-in-Publication Data

McNeill, J. C. (James Calvin), 1905–
    The McNeills' SR ranch.

    (The Centennial series of the Association
of Former Students, Texas A&M University ;
no. 28)
    Includes index.
    1. SR Ranch (Tex.) — History.
2. McNeill, J. C. (James Calvin), 1905–
3. Ranchers — Texas — Biography. I. Title.
II. Series.
SF196.U5M36 1988   636.2'13'09764   88-2204
ISBN 0-89096-340-1

Contents

List of Illustrations

Foreword

It is a rare and delightful opportunity for a ranch historian to review the history of a family-owned noncorporate ranch like the SR of Blanco Canyon. Generally, the story of West Texas ranching has been that of the big spreads—the Matador, Swenson, Pitchfork, Spur, Slaughter, XIT—and so forth. But for every big ranch's history, there lie untold the stories of many smaller operations, whose owners faced the same weather problems and price collapses as did their bigger neighbors. Furthermore, the individual rancher frequently lacked capital reserves or alternate financial resources available to the larger ranches. For that reason, many individually owned ranches could not survive the cold weather of the 1880s, the droughts of the 1890s, or the cattle depression following World War I.

But the SR survived. Primarily because of the frugality of its founder and owner, Captain J. C. McNeill, and because of the dedication and hard work of its resident managers, the SR has lasted for more than a century. Few other families in the Southwest can boast of maintaining land ownership over such a long time.

The story of the SR is a valuable contribution to our better understanding of success and failure in the ranching business. Furthermore, the ranch's longevity makes it a notable study because so few businesses have matched its accomplishment. Also, its history is important because its early history is closely entwined with that of its neighbor, the short-lived Kentucky Cattle Raising Company, or Two Buckle Ranch. The Two Buckle's enigmatic history has yet to be told, but when it is, we will recognize that the contrast between the conservative operation of the Texas-owned SR and the extravagance of the Two Buckle is a great lesson in Great Plains economics.

Finally, the SR's history is especially valuable because of its author, J. C. "Cap" McNeill III. Born on the ranch in Blanco Canyon in 1905, Cap experienced firsthand the majority of the ranch's history. His vivid recollections, coupled with his keen intellect, have produced a personal history similar to, if not better than, Frank Hastings's classic, *A Ranchman's Recollections*.

I became an admirer of Cap McNeill long before I ever met him. While visiting the Margaret Elliott Museum in Spur, Texas, I was intrigued with the following inscription on the wall of the museum:

> There is no present time.
> The transition from the future to the past is instant.
> We have no means for measuring it.
>
> That which we call the present is nothing more than the immediate and reasonably predictable future plus the recent and fully recollected past.
>
> But the future, imminent though it may be, is an unpredictable anticipation. Powers and influences natural or human, alter the plans and expectations of the wise and foolish alike. "The best laid plans of mice and men go often wrong."
>
> Only the past is real, and even that reality is too often lost as recollection fails us, as we neglect the record of event, or as we discard the mementoes representing the lives and accomplishments, not only of those who have gone on before us, but also the earlier phases and occurrences of our own lives.
>
> Let us devote ourselves to the preservation of this only reality in time, that the efforts, sacrifices, and achievements of the past are not wasted.

The author of the inscription was one who loved history, I thought, someone like a Thomas Carlyle, or other great historian. I turned to my host, the Spur Methodist pastor Eddie Allsup, and asked, "Who wrote this?"

Eddie, who was Cap's pastor, proudly replied, "Cap McNeill."

Cap's words, written at the time for a museum dedication, succinctly express what others have tried to say in many pages of writing. Like many ranch people, Cap has always been sensitive to history, but his understanding of the *importance* of history exceed that of many academicians. Now, at the age of eighty-one, he has written the SR story, and in so doing, has provided for us an inspiring account of a family's struggle to make a home in West Texas. He has also lived up to his own admonition to preserve the past in order that "the efforts, sacrifices, and achievements of the past are not wasted."

DAVID J. MURRAH
Texas Tech University, Lubbock

Preface

To the reader of ranch histories, it may appear that those which have been written were about the outfits of great size, but any suspicion of snobbery must take into consideration the availability of dependable information about events, conditions, and operations — especially those occurring in the preceding century. The ownership of the large ranches that endured over a significant period involved nonresidents, generally living at a distance. This situation created correspondence between the absentee owners and resident management, whether employees or part owners. Moreover, the size of these enterprises required acceptable financial records, and these, in combination with surviving letter files, provide the historian with material for a competent account of the ranch's operations and personnel.

Naturally, this situation seldom occurred in smaller ranches, for the owner was usually the resident manager also, leaving a minimal record of his operations and experiences. As a relatively small ranch, the SR was an exception, for the founder and owner never made it his home, spending no more of his time there than was necessary, and none of it in the latter twenty-two years of his ownership. Also, the fact that his home and his ranch were separated by the width of the state of Texas at a time when electronic communication was not available offered no alternatives to the existing postal services.

The absence of any files or actual system of preservation creates some gaps in this resource, but enough has survived to provide sufficient information for a credible story. A boon to the researcher of these old letters lies in the practice of the founder/owner who, although he perforce wrote in longhand, made and saved for himself copies of the letters he considered especially important. Also, the fact that many of his letters concerning the ranch and its personnel were written to family members has provided sources of additional information.

My own lifelong association with the ranch, most of it residential, has been utilized extensively, perhaps too much so, for an excess of autobiography may have intruded. For this I apologize, asking the reader's tolerance of one who is deeply involved in the subject and its principal characters.

Although my advent on the scene was subsequent to the open-range situation existing in 1883 when my grandfather arrived with his cattle at the COE Spring in Blanco Canyon, my perceptive years accumulated early recollections that are indicative of the conditions prevailing when grass covered virtually all the land. By the same token, my observations have included the changes occurring with the arrival of railroads and the farmers and tradesmen who came with them. Those arrivals changed pastures into fields, towns, laned roads (often paved), and other developments that brought about abandonment of once-familiar cow trails and roundup grounds.

But the character of the terrain that includes the SR range has protected the grasslands, for a zone lying below the Cap Rock is, for the most part, too hilly and rough to attract the plowman. As a demonstration of this geological influence, when standing on my porch and looking south, I cannot identify any cultivated fields in the panorama before me, although it extends a full forty miles.

Of course, this expanse of ranch land is not maintained throughout the Cap Rock's progress across Northwest Texas, but however varying its width, it constitutes a grazing reserve that has endured and will probably continue to do so. Therefore, my immediately visible surroundings have not changed much from my childhood to the present, and however great the alterations in many local practices may be, the basic usage of the ranches remains essentially the same.

True, the prairie dogs are gone from our pastures, with their shrill warnings of intruders in their domain, but in the twilight coyotes still speak to one another in tones varying from mournful to ecstatic, and quail signal their locations from covey to covey.

Their messages foster a feeling of rangeland permanence.

I am deeply indebted to Dr. David Murrah, Director, Southwest Collection, Texas Tech University, Lubbock, whose counsel, encouragement, and editorial assistance have been invaluable. As the author of historical books and articles on Texas ranches and ranchmen and given his acquaintance with the vast collection of historical material under his care, supervision, and acquisition, he is particularly qualified as an advisor. This expertise, coupled with congenial friendship and personal support, has provided exceptional guidance for this amateur annalist.

I am also indebted to members of the McNeill family, beginning with my late cousin, L. J. McNeill, Jr., who initiated the whole process with the donation of letters and papers accumulated by our grandfather, Captain J. C. McNeill, Sr. That unsorted collection filled two five-gallon lard cans that had been stored in the basement of the old home on the San Bernard River, and its examination, classification, and evaluation so engrossed me that often the real objective was almost overlooked.

Kerrville author and friend Betty Casey has assisted with advice, critique, and encouragement.

My immediate family has also supported the project and assisted with matters involving reminiscence and recollection. Son George has produced letters and old photographs by rummaging through unlighted and jumbled closets at the ranch house. Assistance in typing has been provided by daughter-in-law Ophelia, a highly significant contribution to the progress of the project.

I am also indebted to family members Sarah McNeill Kelso and Mary Eloise Dance McNeill for contributions of photographs and historical information about the McNeill family, and to my wife, Maude Clemmons McNeill, whose sharing of our ranching experiences has made them endurable in the difficult times and all the more enjoyable when things went well.

The McNeills' SR Ranch

1. The Place

When, following the Civil War, the grasslands of the Southwest became available to those who could use them, cattle raising offered possibilities attractive to many seeking opportunities in a devastated Southland. Although hampered by frontier circumstances, the uninhabited prairies of Texas offered a resource — grass — at no cost to the cowman, and the "machines" — cattle — were readily available to convert that resource into beef, for which there was a strong demand in northern and eastern states. Moreover, these "machines" possessed an additional merit in that they provided their own transportation to the market or railhead. And, largely unattended during the war, they had multiplied into a huge surplus in Central and South Texas.

Cattle prices soared at principal markets, and low costs of production, coupled with skyrocketing values, made fortunes for those who had gotten into the business early and attracted the attention of many who had not. The demand for cattle in the 1860s and 1870s was not limited to supplying beef for American tables, but was enhanced by a rush to obtain herds for stocking newly opened ranges found suitable for cattle raising. The result was a stampede of investors — national and international — falling over one another to get into the cattle business. In the late 1870s and extending a few years into the next decade, this expansion of the cattle-raising industry spread into an area of Texas that was not unknown, but had been unused by any permanent enterprises. This is on or adjacent to the Llano Estacado or "Staked Plains" of Texas.

The perimeters of the region are vague, and to this day it has yet to acquire a title that fully describes or identifies it. It is not a part of the Texas Panhandle, which lies to the north, and the name West Texas identifies the country beginning about San Angelo and extending toward El Paso. Labels such as South Plains and Rolling Plains apply only to sections within the area, so the whole of it has yet to acquire a collective title. Although the events narrated herein focus on Crosby County, they also involve this larger region that

3

originates as a fringe of the Staked Plains and extends south and east from that flat tableland. East and west boundaries loosely outline a territory drained by tributaries of the Brazos River, particularly those culminating in the Clear Fork of that stream.

Measured from the Gulf of Mexico, the most extended reach of these Brazos tributaries has its Texas entrance in a gentle depression near Bovina in Parmer County. Known locally as Running Water Draw, it follows a southeasterly course through Castro, Hale, and Floyd counties. It serves as a runoff outlet for playa lakes when unusual rainfall fills them to overflowing, and it finally breaks through the calcareous layer of caliche and stone underlying the Staked Plains known as the Cap Rock. As this deeper depression cuts across the southeast corner of Floyd County and into Crosby County, it acquires a new identity. Originally called Catfish Creek by early settlers, the stream became known later as White River.

As this water course emerges from the Staked Plains, over a hundred and fifty miles from its entrance into Texas, the enclosing walls flare back to form a valley some five miles in width, with draws and creeks draining into it from either side, while its own streambed becomes a narrow, rocky canyon. Several of these draws flow with waters escaping from the Ogallala aquifer, released from the overburden of the Plains.

Rimming the upper portion of the valley walls are the exposed caliche stones of the Cap Rock escarpment. This geological phenomenon not only creates a commanding presence in the area, but also provides a dividing line separating two different types of terrain. It is the termination of a mineral hardpan that underlies the Staked Plains, protecting the sediments beneath from erosion and creating the great, level expanse that early explorers found frustrating for its lack of guiding landmarks.

The Cap Rock is marked by declivities, often steep, topped by the rim, which exposure has evolved into rock of solidity varying from crumbling caliche to flinty sandstone. The height of the slope varies, reaching in places a hundred feet or more, and in precipitousness from that of a knoll to spectacular crags. The land below it is identified as the Rolling Plains. The soil is different and of greater variety than the loam prevailing over much of the upper levels. Nearby, these lower levels tend to be rugged, with draws and gullies, some steep and rocky.

Cap Rock country

The area around the Cap Rock was prized by cattlemen for the protection afforded their livestock in wintry weather and for the many springs flowing there. Because of the area's irregularity, it has resisted the plow. This accounts for the continued presence of ranches there, with acreages devoted to farming occurring as one moves farther away from the Cap Rock.

The rimrocked depression through which White River flows before its emergence from the confines of the Plains is known as Blanco Canyon, so called because of the white caliche showing at various places, especially at the point where Crawfish Draw enters from the west and a mound of particular whiteness rises, known as Mount Blanco.

In the past, Mount Blanco identified not only the hill, but also the home and activities of Henry Clay "Hank" and Elizabeth "Aunt Hank" Smith, who came into possession of an unfinished rock house there with several sections of land and several hundred head of cattle through default of a man named Tasker when his grandiose plans for a cattle ranch fell through with Smith as his principal creditor.[1] Smith moved his family to the place in 1878, bringing merchandise from a store, bar, hotel, and livery stable he had operated at Fort Griffin, finding customers among those buffalo hunters still in the area. In 1879 his place was designated a U.S. post office, with Mrs. Smith as the postmistress. The Smith place was the first permanent residence established in Crosby County and became a mercantile, medical, social, and political focal point through the formative years of the region. A granddaughter, Georgia Mae Ericson, still owns a part of the original ranch and makes it her home.

Below Mount Blanco, the valley widens, bounded by the precipitous walls of the Cap Rock. The streambed changes, and the narrow ditch coursing through grassy meadows becomes a sandy waterway, winding between gravelly banks, sometimes steep. This part of Blanco Canyon, with its adjoining reaches, is the stage upon which our story is acted out.

Indians used the canyon and its surroundings in a migratory fashion, moving with the great buffalo herds, from which they obtained many of life's necessities. The Civil War diverted any significant competition, and in the years thereafter the Indians demonstrated active hostility to intrusion on their hunting grounds by anyone suspected of desiring permanent residence or wanton destruction of their livelihood. Military campaigns under Colonel Ranald Mackenzie, begun in 1871, culminated in 1874 when the Comanches were conducted to the reservation in Indian Territory after their final defeat at Palo Duro Canyon. With the Indians subordinated, buffalo hunters moved in, conducting a slaughter of the great, shaggy beasts that was practically complete by 1877. Cattlemen were quick to follow, coming mostly from the central part of the state.

Two routes were available to cattlemen that had not been used by trail herds moving north to Kansas and the railroads. The one principally used was Mackenzie's line of march approaching from the southeast. Early seekers of ranges coming from that direction encountered, in some eastern tributaries of the Brazos, water laden

---

[1] W. Hubert Curry, *Sun Rising on the West: The Saga of Henry Clay and Elizabeth Smith* (Crosbyton, Tex.: Crosby County Pioneer Memorial, 1979), 151.

White River

with gypsum and salt, so they pushed on to the Cap Rock country where springs and creeks fed by the Ogallala aquifer issued sweeter waters.

Seldom used, the other route of entry lay along what came to be known as the Cibolo Trail used earlier by Spanish buffalo hunters (the Spanish name for buffalo is *cibolo*), who came up through the present state of New Mexico in ox-cart caravans from as far away as Chihuahua. Drawn as were the Comanches by the buffalo inhabiting the area, they were tolerated by the Indians because their usage was limited to reasonable consumption and because they brought trade goods with them. This trail and its watering places were little known by Texas cattlemen until in 1878 Coggin & Wylie bought two herds of cattle from John Chisum at Fort Sumner and, putting buffalo hunter Frank Collinson in charge, instructed him

7

Cap Rock country

to drive east on that route until he reached the best range he could find.[2]

To say Collinson found that range in Blanco Canyon would, technically, be incorrect, for his acquaintance with the region had been established during his buffalo-hunting days. He knew where he was going and what he would find when he got there. Later, he located the cattle on what was to become part of the Matador Ranch in Motley County.

Like Collinson, early arrivals found a cattle heaven. The absence of the buffalo allowed the grass to flourish, grazed only by antelope, some deer, and a few bands of wild horses. Also, and unknown to newcomers unacquainted with local weather patterns, rainfall in the late seventies was usually heavy, and continued so for the next few

[2]Frank Collinson, *Life in the Saddle* (Norman: University of Oklahoma Press, 1963), 110.

8

years. Thus, in consequence of light usage and abundant moisture, grazing conditions were ideal. The country was soon stocked, with others moving in from the southeast, occupying the range by informal agreement as to who grazed what and approximately how much, based on the size of the herds they brought and centering around dependable watering places.

What was to become the SR Ranch, there in Blanco Canyon and its environs, was occupied by the Petty brothers, Bill and Ed, who left their brand, COE, engraved on a rock at a spring just across White River from where the original McNeill dugout headquarters would be located. Of four brothers who trailed into this section, one, Peter B. Slaughter, settled on a creek that empties into the present White River Reservoir.[3] Some maps identify the draw as Pete Creek, and it is the location of the present McNeill headquarters. He arrived with his cattle, branded P Lazy S, in 1879. As the curtain came down on the open-range era, he left with a thousand head for a long drive to the White Mountains of Arizona. As the first Texan to penetrate that section of the Southwest, he lent his name to the route he traveled to get there.

The situation found by the free-grass people did not last long, and the open-range era was probably telescoped into a shorter period than elsewhere in the West. Several factors contributed to its brevity. In the first place, as previously noted, Indians delayed the invasion by the cowmen. Moreover, the area had not been traversed by trail drivers, who were intent on markets, not permanent pasturage. They established their routes according to known and dependable watering places, coming out of Central and South Texas headed for the Horse Head Crossing on the Pecos River or Doane's Crossing on the South Fork of the Red, thereby missing the Cap Rock country. The tributaries of the Brazos originating in between terminated too quickly to provide dependable waters across the Staked Plains.

After 1874 Indians seldom ventured into the area. Some obtained permits to hunt the few buffalo remaining; others slipped off the reservation bent on stealing horses, generally avoiding any direct contact with the palefaces. Exceptions brought the placement of Texas

[3] W. C. Holden, *The Espuela Land & Cattle Company* (Austin: Texas State Historical Association, 1970), 32.

Rangers in Blanco Canyon at Camp Roberts in 1879 to discourage further encroachments on the early seekers of free grass.[4]

The termination of the open-range situation was hastened by a rush of investors anxious to get into the cattle business, investors with the means to own not only the cattle but also the land on which they grazed. Texas presented a unique opportunity for such investors to obtain large acreages, for when it joined the United States it retained ownership of public lands within its borders, a privilege not extended to other states, where public lands are the property of the federal government. As a result, the State of Texas used these public lands to obtain or promote things needed for its development, granting lands in lieu of cash. The capitol building in Austin is probably the best-known example of this practice.

Most of the grantees of these lands needed money more than they needed land and quickly put their acquired acreages on the market. This made it possible for investors to purchase large tracts, a key element for accelerating the disappearance of free ranges in this area. Much of the land the users occupied was included in grants made to railroads to encourage construction of lines in settled sections of the state or in grants made to populated counties to promote development of public schools. For the railroads, agencies were soon converting the lands awarded them into cash.

Consequently, avid, would-be cattlemen bought the land occupied by the free-grass operators, often stocking their acquired acres by buying the cattle owned by the displaced cowmen, usually by what was known as "book count and range delivery." This was nothing more than the seller's estimate of his livestock, whereby the buyer usually paid for many more cattle than he actually received. However, some of the free-range men, such as the Slaughter brothers, simply moved on south and west to the other areas where free grass was still available.

A second factor enabling purchasers to possess large tracts was the development and distribution of barbed wire. Without it, ranchers would have had no feasible means for enclosing and defending their acreages. With its introduction, free-grazing privileges were soon terminated.

[4] Crosby County Historical Commission, *A History of Crosby County, 1876–1977* (Dallas: Taylor Publishing Co., 1978), 10.

Thus, by 1882, prospective ranchers could not only own the land but could protect it from intrusion. Such developments attracted to this area buyers from throughout the world, including Captain J. C. McNeill, Sr., of Brazoria County, Texas.

2. Early Owners

James Calvin McNeill, Sr., was born November 4, 1844, in Union Parish, Louisiana, where his father, James Campbell McNeill, and his maternal grandfather, Levi Jordan, owned adjoining plantations near the Louisiana-Arkansas border. In 1848 his father and grandfather disposed of these properties and came to Texas, traveling in wagons with their numerous slaves walking alongside. They established a sugar plantation in Brazoria County, a few miles west of the San Bernard River. The plantation was operated as a joint venture. The two men built their own sugar mill, distinctive among others in the area in that the cane juice was extracted under six-foot rollers, reputed to be the largest in the county.[1]

Calvin McNeill and his younger brother, Charles, served in the Army of the Confederacy during the Civil War, privates in Company C, Brown's Regiment, Texas Volunteers, C.S.A. They saw little action in that conflict, their company's assignments being limited to guarding Union prisoners and patrolling the Gulf beaches to discourage raiders from slipping ashore from blockading Union gunboats.

Reconstruction was a long, drawn-out affair in South Texas. The political situation was for over thirty years at best distorted, at worst chaotic. The oath of allegiance a vengeful U.S. Congress imposed effectively barred most of those who participated in the war on the side of the Confederacy from restoration of citizenship. Unscrupulous men controlled the black vote, and the Freedman's Bureau, organized in 1865 to feed, educate, and help blacks adjust to emancipation, soon became the tool of white scalawags (renegade

[1] James A. Creighton, *A Narrative History of Brazoria County* (Angleton, Tex.: Brazoria County Historical Commission, 1975), 225.

recessionists and extreme Unionists) to make things uncertain and uncomfortable for other white men, who had small assurance of justice in the manipulated courts.

In Brazoria County two unofficial groups of volunteers were organized to maintain a semblance of order. One, called the San Bernard Mounted Rifles, was commanded by Calvin McNeill. Later on, the group and its functions received official recognition, and in 1880 Governor O. M. Roberts signed McNeill's state commission as captain, the title that stayed with him the rest of his life.[2]

In spite of these untoward circumstances, Calvin and Charles McNeill renewed sugar production on the plantation, growing the cane on the Jordan land and reopening the mill. Having lost through emancipation the large labor force required, they leased convicts from the State of Texas for $1.15 per man/day under a procedure available at that time.[3]

Sugar production, though an arduous task under prevailing methods, proved prosperous for the brothers. There is no available record of the number of cane crops they raised and processed, but they evidently prospered to the extent that in a few years they could turn to other occupations that did not require so much diligence and manpower — or the pursuit of escaped convicts through semitropical forests. Calvin McNeill chose cattle raising, probably using the idle cane fields as pasture in addition to the grassland already available to him.[4]

In 1867, he entered into a contract for supplying beef to an unidentified buyer or buyers, a venture that may have gotten him into the cattle business in a serious way. Although identities are lacking, similarities in dates and circumstances suggest that he was contracting with local packers, for about this time a method for shipping fresh beef in vacuum-packed cans was introduced in the coastal area, and in 1870 $100,000 worth of canned beef was shipped from Brazoria County. Equally significant is the fact that between 1870 and 1880 the number of these meat-packing plants in Texas declined from fifteen to three as the industry shifted to Illinois.[5]

Speculation is reinforced when considering that in 1867, Captain

[2] Ibid., 262.
[3] Ibid., 208.
[4] W. D. Green, "A West Texas Ranch Saga" (Typescript, 1955, in possession of author).
[5] Creighton, *A Narrative History,* 270.

McNeill bought all the cattle belonging to Samuel Rowe in order to fulfill his contract, which extended over an unspecified period of years. He also acquired in the deal the SR brand first registered by Rowe in 1857, a brand that has since been handed down through succeeding generations of McNeills.

The termination of his contract approximates the sharp decline in the local meat-packing industry, further supporting the impression that his deal was with one or more of these plants. At any rate, without this market outlet, his herd increased beyond the capacity of the range available to him. In 1881 he corresponded with a William A. Rowan, of the Pleasant Valley Ranch near Liverpool, twenty miles away. Rowan offered to take "2,000 female stock, 1,300 of which shall be mother cows," proposing a three-year contract, pasturage to include "all care, branding, etc." for one-fourth of the calves. Although Captain McNeill did not accept the offer, it is evidence of his need for more pasture room and his exploration of means to acquire such.

No correspondence survives to indicate when or through what means Captain McNeill came into contact with John Duncan of Victoria, Texas, but an acquaintance prior to this point is quite likely. As an agent for the New York & Texas Land Company, a firm engaged in the disposal of land grants in Texas, Duncan is certainly likely to have looked up a man known to be needing a home for livestock.

Whatever may have been the preliminary events, as of October 24, 1882, Duncan transferred title to Captain McNeill on eight thousand acres of land in Crosby County, Texas, an undivided one-half of twenty-five 640-acre, odd-numbered (1 through 49) sections in a fifty-section tract designated Block 28, a grant made to the Houston & Great Northern Railway Company. The price was $2 per acre—$8,000 down and a note for an additional $8,000—payable to the New York & Texas Land Company, for whom Duncan acted as agent.[6]

On the same date, Duncan transferred title to the remaining one-half of these odd-numbered sections to the Kentucky Cattle Raising Company, a Louisville corporation newly organized to engage in the cattle business in Texas.[7] Who was contacted first, McNeill

---

[6]Crosby County, Texas, Deed Records, vol. 3, p. 496.
[7]Ibid., vol. 3, p. 326.

or the Kentuckians, and what the first purchaser had in mind by taking only one-half of each section is not known. The fact that the deeds were recorded on the same date has little bearing on the preliminaries to the transactions, and we can only guess at the actual circumstances. The readiness of the Kentucky Cattle Raising Company to buy land thereafter (they wound up with some 140,000 acres) might indicate that Captain McNeill was the preliminary purchaser, but there is no information at all as to the proposition Duncan made to him.

Considering that at this point none of the land in the area had been fenced (actually, little of it had been sold in 1882), it appears probable that Captain McNeill was the preliminary purchaser and that he bought the land as a means of access to badly needed grazing land, possibly in anticipation of a continuance of open ranges. What information remains as to early dealings with the Kentucky Cattle Raising Company, plus correspondence in the next few years, indicates that they wanted to buy him out, and failing to do so, proposed a verbal agreement for joint occupancy, the specifics of which suggest that the captain held the upper hand in their negotiations.

However that may be, in 1883 he shipped fifteen hundred head of cattle to Albany, Shackelford County, Texas, by railroad, which had penetrated to that point in 1881.[8] From thence the herd was driven the 150 miles to COE Spring on the White River. Before being turned loose on the range the cattle were branded with a C in addition to the SR, a device adopted to designate the county in which the cattle belonged should they stray so far from home that the owner's brand might be unknown.

The Kentucky Cattle Raising Company was organized by men primarily engaged in the operation of a distillery in Louisville, producing "Belle of Vernon, Old Fashioned Hand Made Sour Mash Whiskey." They incorporated the cattle-raising venture separately, financing it by the sale of bonds. Officers of the corporation included H. J. Tilford, president; James W. Pirtle, vice-president; Robert J. Tilford, secretary; and C. M. (Claude) Tilford, resident manager.

[8] Walter Prescott Webb, ed., *The Handbook of Texas* (Austin: Texas State Historical Association, 1952), I, 25.

John Tilford also lived at the ranch, where he was listed as resident secretary and weather observer and performed the role of bookkeeper. He was succeeded by John Viley, an in-law of the Tilfords, who was, of all those connected with the operation, the only one with whom Captain McNeill formed a lasting friendship. They corresponded until Viley's death some forty years later.

The Kentucky Cattle Raising Company bought cattle locally from free-grass people, some herds of relatively recent arrival. Major Willa Viley Johnson, who had married into the Tilford family, sold them one herd.[9] Johnson had previously bought the cattle from Indian fighter Colonel Ranald Mackenzie, after the herd had been driven from Bell County, Texas, by a group of cattle traders headed by two brothers named Shanklin, partners with three other cowmen, Casaway, Tomlinson, and Twyman.[10] Payment was made according to the book count practice in vogue with uninitiated newcomers; the three transactions of the transfer, involving Shanklin et al., Mackenzie, and then Johnson, would indicate pumped-up prices as well as a distended count.

The Two Buckle brand the Kentuckians adopted evolved when they bought a herd put together in Central Texas by Pink Higgins, who had branded the cattle "30" as a road brand before driving them to Crosby County. On delivery, a bar was drawn through the "∅" and the "3" was subsequently changed to a "2" for some unknown reason. Thereafter, Two Buckle became not only the identification of the cattle, but also the name by which the ranch was usually known.

The firm continued buying land, purchasing, in time, the even-numbered sections of school land in Block 28, issuing additional bonds to cover the costs. Sales of bonds in 1885 and 1889 totalled $120,000. Crosby County records do not reveal the total of bonds issued, since the initial financing occurred prior to the company's locating in Texas.[11]

Information about initial arrangements for joint occupation of the land is scanty, but Captain McNeill made a trip to Louisville

[9] Undated copy of letter, J. C. McNeill, Sr., replying to the letter from H. J. Tilford, President, Kentucky Cattle Raising Company, dated December 21, 1887. Unless otherwise noted, all references to letters are from the McNeill family papers in possession of the author.

[10] Green, "A West Texas Ranch Saga."

[11] Crosby County, Texas, Deed Records, Vol. 1, p. 211.

to discuss the situation and returned feeling that the adjustment agreed on would require his spending a minimum of his time at the ranch.[12] His Crosby County venture had been entered into as a sideline, designed to permit him to hold cattle in a rising and expanding market.

At the outset, it appeared he had a setup that would allow him to achieve this end without neglecting his family and his varied interests in Brazoria County. He had married Sarah Reese in 1875, and of the eight children eventually born to them, six were already on hand at his home on the Bernard River, a place bought at a tax sale and which had been the home base for James Fannin before he was killed at Goliad during the Texas Revolution.

Captain McNeill established his ranch headquarters in a dugout on Waddell Draw (sometimes called Grape Creek) across the White River from the COE Spring. This type of residence was popular in the area, for the free-grass people had already demonstrated its economical construction and protective efficiency: cool in the summer and warm in the winter. The squeamish might have objected to the dirt and spiders, plus some occasional centipedes and skunks that sought residence there, but most men appreciated the advantages these holes in the ground offered after bedding down outdoors in bad weather.

In Captain McNeill's case, there seemed to be little need for arrangements acceptable to a tidy housekeeper, for he displayed no intentions of spending a great deal of his time at the Crosby County venture. The dugout on Waddell Draw continued to be his headquarters for eleven years. (Significantly, the change occurred only upon the prospect of a female resident, but more about that later.) In these circumstances, the rudimentary accommodations readily available were deemed sufficient for bachelor lodgings. An avid hunter, Captain McNeill was already accustomed to camp life, which he accepted (and enjoyed) as one aspect of outdoor sport.

At the time, and thereafter for a good many years, no social stigma was attached to residence in dugouts, for it was a conventional type of lodging in an area remote from suppliers of lumber and other materials needed for building frame houses, and there was no native timber available in sufficient quantity for building with logs.

---

[12]Letter, J. C. McNeill, Sr., to W. B. Fleming, February 23, 1888.

16

Ruins of SR dugout, 1902. The log ridge pole, visible here, supported log rafters covered with brush and dirt to form the roof. Rocks were used to make a fireplace and the front wall.

Over in Dickens County the Pitchfork Ranch, for example, a cattle-raising venture started earlier and on a much larger scale than the SR, housed their hands in dugouts until 1894, when the first frame structures were erected.[13]

Comparing the operations of the Two Buckle with those of their neighbors is interesting if for no other reason than to illustrate the mania that gripped many investors, domestic and foreign, based on the impression that cattle raising in these newly opened areas was a rapid route to riches and that the current boom would be permanent.

For the Two Buckle owners, dugout accommodations were unacceptable, and by 1885 the Kentuckians were housed in a mansion,

[13] David J. Murrah, *The Pitchfork Land and Cattle Company: The First Century* (Lubbock: Texas Tech Press, 1983), 11.

Bar X ranch house, built by Kentucky Cattle Raising Company, 1884

a two-story building with walls of native stone twenty-one inches thick, located on the White River near falls about five miles north of the Captain's dugout. It was, and still is, a striking location. (The one-time title Silver Falls has fallen into disuse since the cascade itself went into virtual concealment under bridges erected on U.S. Highway 82.) The cost of the house, $4,000, is indicative of practices that would, in a few years, spell the downfall of the Kentucky Cattle Raising Company. This expense may seem insignificant now, but it might be better expressed as the value of at least two hundred cows at the time, or a minimum of about $80,000 in present-day terms, with no additional allowance for plumbing and other modern conveniences.[14]

[14] Nellie Witt Spikes and Temple Ann Ellis, *A History of Crosby County, Texas* (San Antonio: Naylor Company, 1952), 105.

18

Cattle in the early 1880s were accorded a minimum of care and attention, with branding and marketing operations occurring seasonally. This required a minimum of full-time employees, usually one man on the Captain's SR Ranch. Roundups, in season, were cooperative affairs, with extra hands needed for these periods of activity hired only for the duration of the job to be performed. The seasonal use of these extra hands dictated a sketchy schedule of personal economics. Many holed up in towns such as Colorado City, in Mitchell County, or as far away as Weatherford, in Parker County, where relatives might take them in. Some "rode the chuck line," moving from cow camp to cow camp as the limits of hospitality were exhausted.

But these drifting cowboys held no monopoly on uncertainty. The Captain would soon find that his plans for raising cattle in Blanco Canyon were subject to changes brought about by local factors — human, animal, and elemental — that would require more of his time than he had anticipated.

3. Difficulties and Discord

The idyllic situation found in Blanco Canyon in 1883 did not last long. The vagaries of weather that had provided rainy seasons in the preceding years took a dry turn. A combination of blizzards and drought altered range conditions, killing livestock and reducing calf crops. Blizzards drove cattle out of the country as far away as the Pecos River, and many were never recovered by their owners. The blizzard and drought conditions in 1885–86 were not as disastrous in Blanco Canyon as on some neighboring ranches, however. Two things may have contributed to mitigating their effects: the shelter available in the breaks below the Cap Rock under blizzard conditions, and the actual number of cattle on the range.

Typically, the weather and the cattle market followed corresponding regressive trends. An expansion of the national cattle population, paralleling that in Crosby and adjacent counties, brought on an oversupply of beef in the market, and steers that sold for seven cents a pound in 1882 found a lagging demand at two cents a pound in 1886. By October, 1887, the price in Kansas City and Chicago had dropped as low as one cent a pound, making Texas steers almost worthless after freight, yardage, and commission charges had been deducted from the gross price.

In October, 1886, sixty-three SR steers weighing about 825 pounds sold in Chicago at $2.60 a hundred weight, for a total of $1,348.30. The total expense, including freight, amounted to $417.56, or about 31 percent of the gross. The net return to the Captain was $14.77 per head. In June, he had sold a smaller bunch from the Brazoria County place that netted him only $4.84 apiece.

Fencing of the ranges got under way generally in 1884, and the Kentucky Cattle Raising Company was among those which started enclosing their holdings. There is no record to indicate that Captain McNeill participated in this activity, so it seems safe to conclude that fencing was not part of his early arrangements with the Tilfords.

Ranches sought to construct their first fences around the perimeters of their properties, sometimes sharing costs with owners of adjacent lands. The size of the undertaking, the difficulty of obtaining materials, and, in many places, the nature of the terrain left many gaps in these early barriers that were slow in closing. It was a matter of years before various ranches were adequately separated. Some fences were poorly constructed and of inferior materials, and the inclinations and dispositions of the cattle were such that they were quick to take advantage of any discrepancies.

On May 5, 1886, C. M. Tilford, resident manager of the Two Buckles, wrote the Captain: "The roundup will reach our pasture in a few days. . . . I hope this season will see all your cattle as well as ours inside the fence. Send up your horses as quickly as possible. We need them very badly." This indicates that the Two Buckle pastures had been fully enclosed. A carload of horses was shipped by rail from Brazoria County to Colorado City for the spring branding.

Even after fencing, pasture size made it impossible to gather all the cattle in one roundup. Actually, during the next few years so many cattle were still to be found on neighboring ranches that accuracy in a cattle tally was hardly feasible. This prevailed even after general roundups in the open-range style were no longer conducted. Ranches found it necessary to provide "stray men" with their neighbors' crews to accumulate and bring home the cattle that had in-filtrated adjacent pastures. The cattle were wild and unruly, and, according to Captain McNeill, the Two Buckle cowboys' tactics in handling them tended to make them more so, possibly intensifying their inclination to wander.[1]

The Captain knew how many cattle he brought to Crosby County. But because of the circumstances and practices mentioned, his future estimates of the number of cattle he owned relied on a local formula based on the number of calves branded: four older cattle — cows, heifers, steers, and bulls — for every calf.

Evidently the owners of the Two Buckles operated under a false impression that their herd was larger than it actually was. On December 12, 1885, H. J. Tilford wrote to Captain McNeill from Louisville: "We have been disappointed in our expectations about the sale of cattle this month. We had the idea that we should sell 500 head, but Claude has brought in 140 head, as we have learned by telegram."

In 1886 Captain McNeill and the Kentucky Cattle Raising Company became embroiled in long, drawn-out negotiations over the payment of the Captain's eight-thousand-dollar note to the New York & Texas Land Company. The course of communications might be hard to trace even if the file were complete; apparently distances separating those involved and the condition of the current postal system aggravated misunderstandings.

It appears that the officers of the Kentucky Cattle Raising Company harbored misgivings about the Captain's payment of the note. Thus, since it constituted a lien on the odd-numbered sections of which they were joint owners, they paid his note when they paid their own. Their misgivings seem to have been premature, and, when notified of their action, the Captain wrote H. J. Tilford on January 20, 1886, stating that he was ready to reimburse them, but requesting that he be sent the cancelled note with a statement of any additional expenses incurred.

At this point complications developed. Apparently Tilford did not have the note, nor was it in the possession of the New York & Texas Land Company, to whom payment had been made. It appears

[1] Letter, J. C. McNeill, Sr., to H. J. Tilford, January 6, 1888.

that as negotiable paper it had been passed to others, and letters called forth by the situation involved H. J. Tilford in Louisville; John Duncan in Victoria, Texas; C. Anson Jones in Houston; Farmers Loan & Trust Company in New York; American National Bank in Dallas; Ira C. Evans for New York & Texas Land Company in Austin and Palestine, Texas; and Captain McNeill and his lawyer, H. Masterson, in Brazoria.

Months elapsed before the matter was finally settled, and that not until tempers had been ruffled and hard feelings created, some of which could have been avoided if certain financial institutions had not taken weeks to answer their mail.

Discord created by this frustrating business heated up when Captain McNeill received a letter from H. J. Tilford dated January 10, 1887, relative to the sale of the sixty-three steers previously described. The shipment had been made without informing the Captain, who was at his home in Brazoria County, and settlement was made to the Kentucky Cattle Raising Company, with the SR cattle a separate item in the commission company's account of sales.

Tilford wrote, in part:

> Your branding and other indicators indicates that you have upwards of 2,000 head of cattle upon our joint property. . . . The expense for caring for same . . . makes it $1.00 per head. Therefore we debit you with 18 months expenses on your cattle at $1.00 per head . . . amounting to $3,000. We also have an account against you for interest and expenses incurred in the payment of your note amounting to $244.90 which we sent to Mr Masterson. . . . The amount due us after crediting you with the proceeds of 63 head of cattle is $2,293.83, which you can settle by note at 6 months from the 15th with interest at 7%.

The Captain was careful to make a copy of his handwritten reply, dated January 18, 1887:

> I can not for a moment entertain your proposition for me to pay you for running my cattle, for our understanding was exactly the reverse from that and it was your own proposition which was accorded by me. . . . I have furnished horses and hands to help with our cattle and pasturage for mine to run on. My positive instructions to Mr. Claude Tilford last June when I was at the ranch were not to ship any

of my steers and not to sell unless he could find purchaser to take all steers 3 years old and up at twenty dollars a head.

I will ratify your act in selling the 63 head of steers only upon one condition: that you send me the money or exchange on some bank in Texas for it within 30 days from this date.

Hoping for an early and satisfactory answer to this, I am, very respectfully. . . .

The Captain collected his money, and the $3,000 charge was cancelled on the strength of a previous agreement that had been signed June 30, 1885, confirming and clarifying the arrangement worked out verbally in Louisville before either party had located any cattle on Block 28. It read as follows:

> Henry J. Tilford, Prest.,
> Kentucky Cattle Raising Co.
> Dear Sir:
> I desire to cooperate with your company in the management of my business on this range. I will pay my pro-rata part of reasonable expenses and will expect you to care for my cattle as you do your own. I will not lease my range to any one or give the privilege to any one to run cattle with me or lease my lands to any one.
> In consideration of not leasing and co-operating with you, I claim the privilege of using jointly with you, your entire range as though it was my own for five years.
> Witness: Signed:
> C. M. Tilford   J. C. McNeill
> Geo. T. Clarkson   Kentucky Cattle Raising Co.
>   By: H. J. Tilford, Prest.

Two items stand out in the relationship between Captain McNeill and the officers of the Kentucky Cattle Raising Company. In the first place, their joint ownership of the twenty-five sections in Block 28 as undivided interests was an error loaded with potential for problems, problems that might have been avoided had titles to the land specified in some way that each owned a particular half of these 640-acre tracts — "North Half-South Half" — or some sort of legally effective description. Had this been done, the muddle arising out of final payments to the New York & Texas Land Company, involving separate obligations on jointly owned property, might never have occurred, and the rancor generated by one party attempting,

23

for self-protection, to attend to the other party's affairs without adequate previous communications might never have been aroused.

This matter of undivided interests had been and continued to be ignored by each. The fine house and improvements erected by the Kentucky Cattle Raising Company at Silver Falls was on land in which Captain McNeill owned a half interest, as was the "Stag House" built for the cowhands. Likewise, in 1894 when Captain McNeill established ranch headquarters on Section 19 of Block 28, fencing that section for a horse pasture and building a house there, the Kentucky Cattle Raising Company or their creditors owned a similar undivided half interest in the land.

The second item subject to misunderstanding was in the interpretation either might make of the term "reasonable expenses" as used in the operating agreement drawn up in 1885. The operations of these two "co-operators" indicate that their separate ideas of what expenses might be classified as "reasonable" were a long way apart.

In this raw, rough frontier situation, people, for the most part, led raw, rough lives. Captain McNeill's ancestors came from the island of Barra in the Hebrides off the northern coast of Scotland, and their frugal ways were his. His idea of ranching was to operate at minimum expense with no frills attached, and this same system, if it can be designated as such, was largely practiced by his Crosby County neighbors in the 1880s and 1890s. The current life-style of the average cowboy reflected this viewpoint, and his chuck wagon menu sometimes included more sow-belly than beef, his "hot roll" often a couple of old "suggins" (quilts) with a scrap of canvas for its protection.

The Two Buckle outfit was not so frugal. An SR cowboy was amazed to see a Two Buckle hand ride up to their chuck wagon in the middle of the afternoon, dig out a quart can of peaches, cut out the top, eat what he wanted, and throw the rest away.[2] Officers of the company, visiting the ranch during branding, concluded that the hard-twisted manila ropes added to the discomfort of the calves, so on their return to Kentucky they shipped a huge quantity of limp, loose-twisted hemp for which the Two Buckle hands could find little or no use and which they made no attempt to salvage.

[2] Verbal reminiscences, George Williamson to J. C. McNeill III, ca. 1918.

These owners must have been infected with amazing enthusiasm for ranching, but their inexperience cost them dearly. They bought purebred bulls, then overfed them to the extent that many died when turned out on the range. They conducted a well-drilling program whose cost effectiveness was questionable and made other improvements with scant regard to expense when the cattle business was in the doldrums, operating all the time on money borrowed through the sale of short-term bonds. Throughout, their income never matched expenses.

On December 28, 1885, H. J. Tilford wrote to Captain McNeill: "I have spent a little over $200,000 in Texas since I saw you and we have only sold 90 beeves which brought only 3½¢ [a pound]." They seem to have paid little heed to this early warning, breaking out grassland in 1884 and 1885 for a farming venture, planning to raise feed. Local settlers did the work at exorbitant rates, and the land was never properly cultivated and soon failed to fulfill the owners' dreams of cheap feed for their steers.[3]

Toward the end of 1887, communications with the leadership of the Kentucky Cattle Raising Company were reopened by a letter from H. J. Tilford dated December 21 and addressed to the Captain at his Brazoria County home. Tilford's letter and the Captain's response illustrate the contrast in their views on ranch management.

> The sale of beeves this fall convinces us that we must at once infuse new blood into our herd . . . and we write to ask if you do not think it would be a wise step to buy one hundred to one hundred and fifty thorough-bred Short Horn or Hereford bulls and if you would not like to join us in this purchase. . . .
>
> We see no hope to ever realize a profit on our investment, except to pursue such a course as this and furthermore to farm upon a large scale and feed our steers before shipment. . . .
>
> We would be very glad to have you join us in the purchase of bulls and some other improvements which we are contemplating.

The Captain responded promptly and at some length.

> I am glad to hear from you on a business that we are both interested in. . . . Your idea about the bulls is a good one. . . . Your [previous] importation of young thoroughbreds proved a failure, not more

---

[3]*A History of Crosby County, 1876–1977*, 104.

than 20 passed through the first winter alive, and some have died since. . . .

I am not easily convinced that farming can be profitably conducted on the plains and that food for cattle can be raised at small cost . . . better let the farmer raise the grain and the stock man raise the cattle. . . . I have sold . . . in the past four years $9,000 worth of cattle and am paying taxes on 1900 head this year. . . .

This summer there was fully 4000 stray cattle taken out of your pasture [and] there is still several thousand strays remaining. . . . Remove these strays, turn out or purchase plenty of bulls, cut down and keep well posted. . . .

Shanklin used to work three men and those men were interested in the stock, each owning cattle. . . . You worked from fifteen to twenty men this year [and] had 150 horses . . . and your expenses must be great.

The company was also ahead of the times when in 1887 it laid out a town site in Blanco Canyon and named it St. Ulrick.[4] Efforts to interest a number of Scotch families in Edinburgh were fruitless, and not a one of the Scotchmen ever visited the proposed municipality. A second attempt was made at a different site in 1890 and likewise failed. Such ventures could not succeed at such a distance from rail service.

The 1880s were, for the most part, trying ones for the Captain. The cattle market had gone sour, the weather had taken an unfavorable turn, and his working arrangement with the Kentucky Cattle Raising Company had fallen apart. He was forced to spend much more of his time at the ranch than he had planned, finding no one competent to look after his interests there on a year-round schedule.

His extended absences from his home and family were painful for himself, his children, and his devoted wife Sarah, whose letters reveal anxiety and desolation while he was away. By 1887 their family had grown to eight children of their own; in addition, their home, known as Liberty Hall, extended a welcome to friends and relatives who came for visits ranging from a few hours to years.

Sarah wrote him frequent newsy and loving letters, always lament-

[4] Ibid., 105.

Liberty Hall, Captain McNeill's Brazoria County home

ing his absence and yearning for his return. The Captain responded frequently and affectionately; correspondence was their only means of communication, and they made full use of it, despite delays in getting the mail to and from the railroad at Quanah, in Hardeman County, via a horse-drawn hack. He received many letters from the children, too, particularly the older girls, and complained when a ride to the post office at Dockum's store failed to produce any news from home.

For the McNeills, the pains of separation only added to the dismal situation in Blanco Canyon, as indicated by Sarah's letter of October 4, 1887: "Take care of your precious self for my sake and try to over come your worries. . . . The old adage 'It is always darkest just before day'. . . . I hope it is with us."

The adage may have been demonstrated in the end, but for the Captain the darkest hours were still ahead of him.

4. Death, Drought, Die-offs

The Captain's response to Henry Tilford's invitation to join in the purchase of bulls included, as we have seen, some pointed advice. But, other than approving the idea of using purebred bulls, he neither accepted nor rejected the proposition. His lack of confirmation may have been taken as rejection by the Two Buckle management and treated as such. At any rate, there followed a chain of unusually rapid correspondence. Only three of the letters are available now, but the gist of the missing ones is obvious.

The series was evidently initiated by a suggestion by the Kentucky Cattle Raising Company of separation in place of cooperation. On February 10, 1887, James S. Pirtle, vice-president, wrote a letter that clearly indicated previous communication.

> I have received your letter proposing an effort to make division of lands in Crosby County, Texas, owned by yourself and the Kentucky Cattle Raising Co. jointly, by agreement rather than by reference to arbitrators, as suggested by us.
> We are willing to make an effort to divide the lands by consent. . . . We own . . . all the sections of even numbers [school land] in Block 28. How would it suit you to have us offer some of our even numbered sections for your interest in some sections owned jointly? It may be to our mutual interests to get lands in a body instead of small parcels.

This was evidently followed by a letter dated February 14, 1888, from a W. B. Fleming, whose connection with the Kentucky Cattle Raising Company is not apparent, but with whom the Captain seems to have had a friendlier relationship than with the Tilfords. On February 23, 1888, the Captain replied:

> Your favor of the 14th to hand for which I am grateful. . . . You I have full confidence in, and would only be too glad to meet you . . . [but] I have neither the time nor inclination to visit Louisville just now and am waiting for your company to formulate plans for division of our undivided interests in Crosby County. I am perfectly willing to divide. State your proposition and will quickly answer.

Reply to the Captain's letter came from Pirtle, dated March 29, 1888, and included a proposal whereby exchanges of ownership in jointly owned sections plus adjoining school lands would solidify the Captain's holdings in a thirteen-section block. No copy of any answer the Captain may have written in response has been found; it is possible he did not even write one. For, although as Pirtle pointed out in his letter the division would have awarded the Captain an extra 320 acres, the block suggested would have included comparatively undesirable acreage. Most of it would have been above the Cap Rock, plains land low-rated for its lack of permanent watering places and protection in wintry weather. Moreover, the small acreage under the Cap Rock Pirtle suggested included none of the spring-fed creeks.

Whether the Captain penned a formal rejection of the proposal or chose to ignore it as unworthy of response, nothing came of it, although one can reasonably suspect that as a result his relationship with the owners of the Two Buckles continued to deteriorate.

For Captain McNeill the "darkest hour" referred to by his wife Sarah in 1887 arrived with her death on May 4, 1890. He had taken her to San Antonio seeking medical aid for her illness, the character of which is not apparent. The finality of her condition and the anticipation of death is evidenced by her children's presence when she died; they had all been taken to San Antonio in order that she might have them with her at the end.

Her death was a terrible blow to the Captain, for theirs was a particularly loving marriage. It also brought him all the responsibilities in which she had been a real helpmeet in his absence, and his presence at home became all the more important. He was left with eight children, three boys and five girls, ages three to fourteen. Her sister-in-law, Frances Reese, agreed to take charge of the household, bringing with her five children of her own. Since the place was already home to three Williamson children, Mrs. Reese had to supervise and teach sixteen active youngsters. Only the assistance of numerous black servants enabled her to handle the job.

Not long after Sarah's death, her nephew, George Williamson, returned from a sojourn in Colmesneil, Tyler County, where he had been working at a sawmill. He was the oldest of the four Williamson children, all of whom spent varying periods of their lives in the Captain's household. Family tradition has it that George went to East Texas to avoid Brazoria County law officers. He apparently shot up the post office in Alvin. He returned after allowing some time for his Alvin antics to fade from official memory, but was soon in trouble again. While assisting with the operation of a ferry, he got into an altercation with a black man, subduing him by hitting him with an oar. He carried the unconscious fellow to the house, where his condition was pronounced grave, perhaps fatal. So George left once again and wound up in San Antonio working in a wood yard.

The Captain now, as never before, needed a dependable representative at the ranch, and George Williamson seemed a possibility for filling this urgent need. Three of the Williamson children, George, Laurance, and Ida, demonstrated deep devotion to him and his wife throughout their lives, and the Captain believed George, given the chance, would prove his loyalty in a responsible position. He wrote to offer him the job, frankly acknowledging its disadvantages, as is evidenced by his nephew's reply:

> Well, about the ranch — I will leave that to you. I am heartily tired of San Antonio, but positively I do not want you to put me to work unless you have use for me, and most positively if I can help you while I am endeavoring to help myself. . . . I know the ranch would be very lonely, but a man had just as well be by himself as with people he has no interest in. I am as much alone here as I would be at the North Pole.

That the arrangement was completed is evidenced by a letter to J. C. McNeill, Jr., dated June 8, 1890, wherein Williamson related his arrival at the ranch and his soreness after three days of helping with the spring branding.[1]

After Williamson's arrival, the Captain wrote to his children on July 3, 1890, describing life at the dugout:

> George is going to the post office. I am going after the horses. Ned [cowhand] is cooking dinner, and whilst waiting will acknowledge your favors about the 23d of June, missent to Mt. Blanco instead of Dockum's [store], Dickens County. Don't send letters to Mt. Blanco, it is twenty miles off. . . . Glad to hear from you, and note letters from all. . . . Of course you expected me for District Court. Well, I couldn't well come, we were branding calves, have branded to date 423. . . .
> Am expecting to meet some of the stock holders in the Kentucky

---

[1] J. C., Jr., was the only one of the Captain's family who had been to the ranch, sent there by his mother in 1887. He would not return until 1899.

Cattle Raising Co. this week by engagement. What they want I shall not be likely to grant.

Alice, the little squirrel slipped his head out of the string and quit us. He was a beauty, small and spotted. I tried to buy a pet antelope — fellow wouldn't sell or give. Would like so much to take a young antelope home for you children to see.

Sadie, Mr. John Viley sent me down a bag of cat and kittens, and they are mewing now. Some of the kittens are quite pretty.

The skunks and tarantulas run us out of the dugout, and we built a shade up the hill and sleep in swinging beds made of barrel staves and rawhide.

It rained a splendid rain last night and is threatening to rain again.

M. E. [Mary Emily] we have got eleven calves in the pen and have milk at our meals. The cows are wild and takes work to handle them — think we will have to turn some loose and try to find gentler ones.

George ain't a nice housekeeper. Dinner is hot coffee, cold biscuits, cold meat and sweet milk.

Now for the saddle and good bye. Will write again soon or come home — don't know what will be the next move, depends on circumstances. . . . Affectionately. . . .

The mail delivery problem stemmed from the fact that when the Captain first came to Crosby County, Mount Blanco was the nearest post office, but in 1885, when a star route was established to carry the mail from Colorado City to Estacado, Dockum's store became the post office.[2] This was only about seven or eight miles east of the dugout.

The early branding completed, the Captain returned to his home and children, leaving Williamson in charge with one cowhand to help. A letter dated July 21, 1890, reports on conditions and circumstances. It also indicates how widely cattle were dispersed in spite of the fences that had been erected. Roundups had to cover four counties: Crosby, Dickens, Motley, and Lubbock. Williamson wrote:

Ned and I went to Mt. Blanco yesterday to church. Saw H Bar L [St. Louis Cattle Company] man. They commence work tomorrow [and] Ned will go up today. H Bar L got only four SR cattle out of Matador range, two cows and two yearlings. Curlin told me he got only nine Two Buckles, so I guess we haven't any more there, if any.

H Bar L report no water between here and Amarillo except at

[2] Fred Arrington, *A History of Dickens County* (Privately printed, 1971), 240.

windmills and Tool [Tule] Canyon. It hasn't rained a drop since you left, grass is curing up very fast. Water nearly all gone on plains. . . . Cattle come to creek [White River] in droves and in a long trot. Wouldn't be surprised if beef [steers] aren't just about as good [fat] as they are going to get.

Two Buckles don't know when they will work again. Some talk of not working before September, but I think surely will work before then.

Had quite a [prairie] fire out close to Estacado, was still burning yesterday, but not burning much judging from the smoke.

Saw Igo, Z Bar L boss, yesterday and he says he thinks the one-eyed mare is in their range. Ned will find out before he gets back.

John Viley just passed and says Catfish [White River] was dry down about Pole Hollow. You have no idea how things are drying up.

A letter dated August 11, 1890, illustrates again the distances a Crosby County rancher would have to travel to look after his cattle.

As you see, I am at Dockum. Learn here that Spurs will commence work on 15th of this month if [A. T. "Bud"] Campbell gets back, if not, as soon as he does. . . .

Saw Curlin yesterday, said if I would find out about Spur work he would find out about IOA. They propose to work from Yellow House [Canyon] between 25th and 28th of August.

Jim Dalton [Two Buckle foreman] . . . will be gone till about 1st of September, and will work [all that range].

I wish you were here. I don't like to act on my own responsibility, but if Ned is gone to Lampasas he will hardly get back [in time for Spur work].

I know we ought to go in west side of Spurs. . . . They will begin on McDonald [Draw]. Just the place for us.

We have no record of just what proposition representatives of the Kentucky Cattle Raising Company made during a visit in July, 1888, but some significant developments occurred thereafter, with telling effects on both co-owners of Block 28.

The Kentuckians built a fence along the south line of the grant, dividing their ranch into two big pastures of approximately the same size, with about a hundred sections in each. Before the fall work started in 1890, they announced plans to defer grazing the south pasture created by the division fence. This they proposed to do by putting all or most of their cattle north of the fence for the winter, reserving the south pasture for grazing in the growing season. They directed the Captain to concentrate all his cattle in the north pasture, pointing out that he had no ownership of acreage south of the dividing line.

On Dec. 7, 1890, Williamson wrote: "Finished work today . . . methinks we have about all the calves [branded], only four calves the last time . . . had to keep working on account of cattle drifting so badly. When you left we had branded 554, since then we branded 57, which makes a total of 611 calves for '90, a little better than we expected."

In large pastures, even as under open-range conditions, cattle tended to establish their individual ranges about watering places, normally limiting the extent of their grazing to areas convenient to water. Thus, in working a range, cowmen attempted to define these water-centered localities and to pattern their drives accordingly.

But as seasons and conditions changed, cattle sought improved circumstances—better protection, better grass, betterment of a deteriorating environment. When this occurred, defining roundup areas became difficult because cattle mixed while searching for improved conditions. Branded and unbranded calves could show up in any given area.

Williamson's friendly relations with the Two Buckles soon changed. Although he usually found manifestations of enmity irritating, on occasion he was amused. He found humor in one incident he related to his uncle—a conversation he had with Claude Tilford, resident manager for the Kentucky Cattle Raising Company.

They had inadvertently sold a two-year-old SR steer, for which the Captain requested reimbursement. Williamson reported in his letter:

> Collected from Tilford O. K. The following is the conversation between CMT [Tilford] and myself:
> 'George, that was only a 2-year-old I carried off.'
> 'Yes, sir.'
> 'I only got $17.50 for my twos.'
> 'Yes, sir.'
> 'This order is for $20.'
> 'Yes, sir.'
> He thinks a while and says:
> 'When John [Viley] comes in I'll give you a check.' John came, took the order and went to write the check. Claude then remarks:

33

'If the old man [McNeill] would pay me all he owes me I would have quite a sum.'

'Does he owe you something, Mr. Tilford?'

'Do you know how many cattle he is allowed by law to keep here?' says he.

Says I: 'No, sir.'

Says he: 'Seven hundred and forty.'

'Well,' I says, 'you ought to collect. Collecting is worth as much as a trade.'

Claude says no more. I smiled in my sleeves.

But Williamson was not amused with Dalton, the Two Buckle foreman.

Jim was very indignant at my not helping throw cattle into the upper pasture. I sent men down to help make the drive. . . . I of course declined to help. First few roundups we attended [thereafter] he was very [angry] and forbid me roping [calves] in the roundup. I told him I caught SR cattle where I found them and asked no odds.

He got in a good humor then, invited me to stay all night at his camp so I would not have to ride so far to the drive. I declined as the dugout was more comfortable, but took care of his men when sent here.

He has since said, 'George, it is against orders for us to mix in any way when working, but what we do is our business. If old man Tilford and McNeill want to fight, let them. We will obey orders and remain friendly, and any way we can help one another without getting ourselves into trouble, we will do.'

My opinion of Jim is when he finds he can't run it over a man, he then wants to chum with him. He is a snake in the grass, Uncle Calvin, a snake in the grass.

Dalton's attempt to prevent Williamson from roping SR calves in the roundup was only a repetition of a situation the Captain had faced a few years earlier. The accepted practice in a general roundup was for a roper from each ranch to look through the herd for calves following cows of his brand, rope them, and drag them out to the branding crew. A member of the Two Buckle staff notified the Captain that their ropers would drag out all the calves, and that it would not be acceptable for him to rope any calves in the roundup, not even his own. They would be brought out to him by a Two

34

Buckle hand. When the Captain went in himself, a Two Buckle rider came to escort him to the outside. We have no record of the conversation that ensued, but the Captain continued roping his calves and sent the Two Buckle rider back to his station.

It seems doubtful that the Tilfords were directly responsible for this, but Dalton's conduct is probably typical of that displayed by other Two Buckle employees hopeful of some prestige in a fancied superior organization. Such larger purpose, and its coarse pursuit by the company's hired men, is indicated in a letter from J. S. Chapman, president of the Denton Land & Cattle Company, dated September 6, 1884. This firm had stocked land north of the Two Buckle, and Chapman suggested a cooperative effort through purchase or lease of the Captain's holdings: "We want to cope with our Kentucky friends, who are endeavoring to control the Canyon."

Unquestionably, the Captain had overstocked his eight thousand acres of grazing land. However, this judgment needs qualification in light of ideas current at the time, for no one really knew the carrying capacity of the grasslands. Overstocking was the general practice, encouraged at the outset by the ideal conditions prevailing when cowmen first moved in with their herds. For example, the Espuela Land & Cattle Company (Spur Ranch), neighbors to the east, had stocked their land at the rate of one cow to every three and a half acres. Perceiving their error, in 1887 they sold more than fourteen thousand head, still maintaining a stocking rate of one cow to every four and a third acres. Time proved this adjustment insufficient, and they suffered heavy die-offs when unfavorable weather caught up with them.[3]

The Captain's previous experience in cattle raising was in a semitropical area where cleared land produced forage at a rate surpassing anything available in Crosby County. Although he was compelled, in time, to modify his ideas about the stocking capabilities of Blanco Canyon, the Captain maintained an inflated opinion of the productivity of his pastures, feeling that any reduction in marketable cattle resulted from poor management, for which his local representative bore responsibility.

However that may have been, the 1890 concentration of SR and

[3] W. J. Elliot, *The Spurs* (Spur, Tex.: Texas Spur, 1939), 31-32.

Two Buckle cattle in the upper pasture would soon demonstrate that it was badly overstocked, and dry weather would cause both occupants to suffer the consequences.

5. Cold War in the Canyon

Of Williamson's letters to the Captain or members of his family, nearly all those which have survived were written in 1890 and 1891. One might reasonably expect that he would write less frequently as he acquired more confidence in his ability to represent his uncle's interests in Crosby County, but undoubtedly many of his letters written in ensuing years have simply disappeared.

Correspondence during these years occurred in a period of significant developments in what Duff Green calls a "cold, undeclaired [*sic*] war" between the Captain and the Kentucky Cattle Raising Company. What he reported to the Captain sheds some light on that situation, however biased his reports may have been. Moreover, the letters portray something of the life and circumstances of a cowpuncher on a comparatively small ranch, hemmed in by giants and working, for the most part, alone, with a minimum of equipment, facilities, and money.

Williamson was blest with a keen sense of humor, a quality that undoubtedly enabled him to offset the isolation, hostility, and frequent difficulties. The letters, through many personal items, also reveal affection for and loyalty to his uncle and his interests, and the comradeship that existed between the two.

The Captain was an indefatigable hunter, maintaining at his Brazoria County home as many as three packs of hounds for the pursuit of bear, deer, and the long-tailed cats (ocelots) then prevalent in the area. Virtually all his kinsmen shared his ardor, so his nephew wrote to an appreciative audience when recounting experiences involving game and guns. Thus, on December 7, 1890, Williamson wrote:

> An antelope ran too close to me the other day on a drive as we
> were throwing the roundup together. I shot him through the kidneys,
> knocked him down and started to him to cut his throat but he got up

36

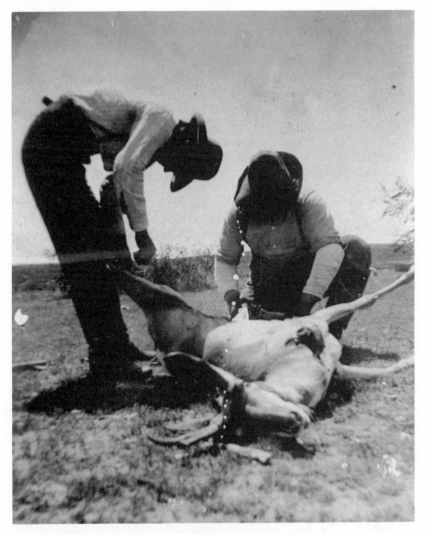

George Williamson and Jim McNeill skinning an antelope, 1902

from there and ran down five horses and then got through the fence and got away. I got one throw [rope] at him but missed. Jim Dalton threw at him three times and Tom Fulcher once but nobody could capture him. . . . The farther that antelope went the better he got.

Let me tell you about my last goat killing. I crawled up in about 90 or 100 yards of them. When I shot, saw but one, balance [of them] in a hollow. When I fired all ran out and my goat looked like all the rest after the bunch came out to him. I shot the one closest to me and knocked him down, only went a few jumps. . . . I went to my dead goat wondering why I didn't kill the first one I shot at, and found I had shot the same goat twice, two holes about two inches apart . . . and both just behind the shoulder.

Now say if you dare that wasn't good shooting and bad luck. While I'm bragging I'll tell you about a shot I made this eve, shot a jack rabbit just 105 steps [away] and don't think I missed where I aimed a half inch. I won't tell you I shot at the same rabbit about half that distance and missed him.

On December 22, 1890: "Rode with Jim all day looking at cattle. . . . I was in search of a cow fat enough and old enough to make beef. . . . Found one . . . and killed her . . . cut up and salted and hung up and now have meat enough and grease [tallow] enough to cook with to last till spring . . . cut in large chunks and will pack [it] in a barrel as soon as it dries out enough. . . . By feeding the dogs with my gun will make it do me for the winter."

He did not enjoy his housekeeping chores, as indicated in a letter dated February 3, 1891: "Am going to fence me a patch . . . and plant some of everything I can think of that a man can eat raw. Don't want anything that has to be cooked. Am full up to my neck of cooking." And on February 14 he reported: "I have my garden fenced, just a little over a half acre. Will borrow a plow soon as grass begins to put up . . . don't know where I will get a plow, don't like to ask the Two Buckles for one [and] hate to go to Mt. Blanco [Hank Smith's] or [Spur Ranch] farm for it but guess I'll have to use one of the three."

Old lists enumerate by names twenty to thirty saddle horses used, but most of these were turned loose in the winter. Two or three would be retained and fed grain as supplement to maintain stamina for frequent usage. Sometimes the grain could be obtained from "nesters"; often it was brought to local supply stores by freighters hauling from railroad points.

Williamson related his grain-hauling difficulties on December 27, 1890:

Got mules in Christmas Day and next day *Friday,* went after my corn. Put it all on intending to haul to Waddell [Draw] . . . go out on the south side of the fence [to avoid rough terrain and get closer to the dugout] and divide [the load, for descent to the camp] and this way make one day do the job.

Now mark how my plans were knocked in the head and say if you dare there is no such things as fate or Friday being an unlucky day. I know it wasn't *bad management.* But have it as you will, just as I came down the hill at Curtis [Creek, about five miles from the dugout] Crash! I looked back and one of the hind wheels was very down, shelled every spoke out as nicely as you could shell a row of corn from a cob.

Well, there I was and there was the corn, too. Borrowed old man [Ed] Hutson's wagon, found it as badly dilapidated as ours, so had to make two loads of it after all. . . . So you see to save one day I lost two. Will take Hutson's wagon home tomorrow.

Another of Williamson's problems was the lack of a small pasture in which to keep his horses. They had to be turned out in the upper pasture (some sixty or seventy thousand acres) in the hopes that they would not stray too far away from the camp. One horse was usually kept penned, but in slack times this practice, too, was occasionally omitted to conserve feed. He lamented this inconvenience in a December 22 letter: "Have been afoot for the past four days. Tried turning my horses . . . loose and got left by it. Two Buckle man came along this eve — borrowed his horse and found them close to the old Boot camp."

On February 2, 1891, he began preparing a solution, reporting it in a letter the next day: "Yesterday I went up on Gannon Draw and wound up about seven hundred yards of wire. Will haul it down first time I get the mules up. Wish I could put in about ten or fifteen acres of feed stuff this year." He did, in time.

Williamson's life in the dugout was not always solitary, as he related December 27: "Well, to finish this page will tell you a skunk story. Old Queen found one by the wood pile the other night. I went out, shot him and came back to bed, and bless dick here he comes with one fore leg shot off. Had gone around the other side of the wood pile and beat me to my own den. I just shot him again, and tonight I can tell there has been a skunk in here just as easy."

Not all his human visitors were welcome, either, especially if they were riders of the chuck line, off-season cowboys such as Tom Stewart. He wrote February 21, 1891:

I have just gotten rid of Tom Stewart. He turned his horse loose with mine and the devils never came up any more. This morn the mules came up and I backed [rode] one and got the horses. To be cooped up [foul weather] is punishment enough, but to have that fellow's company added to it is simply terrible. He hasn't an idea above stealing something. I would have gone to the post office this eve but was afraid the d———n thief would slip [away] and steal some of my blankets. Said he had to be stealing some pretty soon as it wasn't long before work [roundups] would begin.

Sometimes Williamson's visitors were more numerous, as he wrote the Captain February 3, 1891:

Dear Uncle: Well, I am loaded chock full. All the Two Buckle men called on me today. First, John Viley took dinner with me and talked lots. Gives Jim [Dalton] and Claude [Tilford] down grade, Claude especially. Says he heard very indirectly that the Company is going to establish an office in Fort Worth and put C. M. [Claude] there. Says he will do the Company about as much good there as he will here, and that he would do just about as much good in Central Africa as he will there. . . .

John Viley is much put out, says the Company is not only losing on this business but are keeping themselves drained on their Kentucky business. . . .

Well, he blows off, then Dutch John comes, giving Jim the devil. I remarked that Jim had been very clean to me. John says, 'Yes, to your face'.

Just as Dutch John was going Jim rides up, eats his dinner a-swearing Dutch John is not worth a damn and that John Viley is the contrariest man alive.

Well, just as Jim is about done blowing off and is ready to leave, Kid Overhulse, line rider [Spur Ranch] comes, cusses the whole outfit in behalf of Jack who has a Two Buckle check for $230.00 protested on him. Sent the check to a Colorado City bank for collection. Bank sent the check to the Kentucky Cattle Co. and the Company refused to pay, gave no reasons.

This is the second check done likewise lately. 'Now my dear sir (says Overhulse) what are you going to do with such an outfit?' I am listening out loud and do my talking to myself, but once in a while I smile a bit.

John Viley and Jim both predict a light branding and a big die-off later. I 'kinder' agree with them as I can't see how it can be otherwise.

Williamson's opinion of the cattle's condition had apparently changed. Early in the winter of 1890–91, on December 7, he had written hopefully, citing mild weather and reporting that the concentration of cattle in the north pasture seemed to produce no ill effects: "I could shove a good many cattle through the [dividing] fence if necessary but blamed if I don't believe they are doing just as well where they are." But again on December 27, he expressed his resentment of the fence: "I wish I had some kind of acid that would eat a wire in two in a few days by daubing it on once. I could put in so many leisure moments daubing. Wouldn't I laugh to see about five miles of good fence fall down. . . . We are still having delightful weather, clear and cool but not cold. Haven't had any frost for several nights."

Soon adversity materialized, as he reported on January 7: "No water on the plains except at windmills. Cattle continually falling away [in condition] but haven't seen any dead ones. Have seen some though that are sure to go later."

Whatever the Kentucky Cattle Raising Company's objectives may have been, rotational grazing became an all-too-evident mistake. On February 14, Williamson wrote the Captain:

> Weather clear and warm but some cattle passing in their checks, have seen some four or five dead cows. Not an SR yet but no doubt there are some going. . . . Jim stayed all night with me . . . and this morn we tore down the new fence across Catfish [White River] so the cattle could drift down [to the lower pasture]. . . . Jim has opened the fence in a good many places. . . .
>
> Now doesn't that show management? Waited till dead of winter to work just to get to use that fence, [and] now that the harm is done . . . they pull [it] down. . . . Am glad it is done, but if this was to be, why destroy stock one day and remove the destruction the next day, or rather, the last day.

Four days later he reported: "Cattle are dying pretty freely, old cows and last year's calves mostly. Can't see what kills the calves, they are not so poor." And again, on March 6: "Cattle bogging [at watering places] very little. Blamed if I can see what holds some of them up, they are so poor. We are losing lots of calves, they are coming and dying every day. Most of the cows that die either have calves or are about to."

With the beginning of spring branding in 1891, Williamson had completed his first year on his uncle's Blanco Canyon ranch. He had arrived in 1890 in time to participate in the spring branding, and a letter of May 26, 1891, was written just as the annual roundups were getting under way: "Have just finished working the upper pasture. Only branded 100 [SR] calves. Two Buckles began work on the 14th in the lower pasture."

In these roundups the Two Buckle concentrated their steers in the upper pasture and their cows and heifers in the lower pasture. For reasons unknown they avoided having Williamson along while working the lower pasture, as he wrote his uncle: "They didn't notify me of [the] work, but slipped out on me. Then when they got to the upper pasture [where the SR cattle were concentrated] lied to me and caused me to miss one of the largest roundups." These omissions were significant, since gaps in the division fence allowed SR cattle to range in both pastures.

Drought was not the only menace to the cattle. On May 26, Williamson commented: "Am afraid screw worms will injure the calves we branded. Never saw them worse, and wolves . . . are killing calves by the dozen. I have counted at least fifty [carcasses] in the last three weeks, and no telling how many others. We had 36 calves in [the] pen the other day and among them four that wolves had [injured]." Lobo wolves were a menace to cowmen and a boon to coyotes, for they left them the remnants of their kills. Powerful brutes, lobos sometimes killed grown cattle by severing their hamstrings, rendering the animals helpless before continuing the assault.

Williamson's letter of June 19, 1891, reveals his quandary as a small operator surrounded by big ranches at whose roundups he needed to attend to pick up stray cattle. Without a crew from which to draw, he hired extra hands to take part in the neighbors' seasonal roundups, adjusting, as best he could, to the schedules they established and paying particular attention to the times they would be working close by, where SR strays were most likely to be found.

In a letter he outlined his understanding of activities on the Spurs, Matadors, and Two Buckles, with the arrangements he was making to comply. He urged his uncle to make an early appearance at the ranch, indicating some of the difficulties that would accrue should his arrival be delayed. Temporary hands hired as stray men often gave Williamson trouble. They were, for the most part, beyond his control while working with the other ranches, and inclined to use that distance to extend their employment. Range bosses, finding their services helpful and inexpensive, frequently encouraged this practice.

Williamson wrote:

> Joe hasn't come in yet. Don't know what to think of him. I told him positively not to work [the] north pasture of [the] Matadors. . . . I know as sure as I know my name he isn't getting anything [SR strays] now. Can't help being a little fretted with him, he has let some of those thieves talk him into working on 'round because they need hands.
>
> My Yellow House man [SR representative to the IOA roundups] will begin [working there] tomorrow unless he wants to see the country too.

Williamson was probably the first of Captain McNeill's managers to operate with a paucity of funds, but certainly not the last. Letters dated December 31 and January 2 concerned payment of taxes at Estacado and settlement of accounts with the store at Espuela, which left him with only $5.76.

Financially generous with his children and other beneficiaries, the Captain was tightfisted with operating expenses, as indicated in a letter on October 31, 1891: "Will be done [with] work in about seven days, and not a blamed cent to pay hands. . . . I don't like to be continually crying money, but . . . have been looking for some for some time." Williamson enumerated some of the obligations outstanding, principally wages owed extra hands. On November 11 he acknowledged the Captain's response: "Received yours with check for $100.00 enclosed. You can see from my last that it was not enough. Corn is one dollar a bushel in this country."

Williamson's reference to wages owed cowhands indicates the customary manner among cattlemen whereby no set pay day was observed. Instead, during the period of employment the cowboy drew such amounts as his immediate needs required, and purchases were often made for him when someone was going to town or to a country store. The owner or his resident manager kept an account of these withdrawals, and when the term of employment ended, the total wages due were calculated, the charges against them deducted, and the balance paid, usually by check.

This custom was typical in areas where banks were far apart and the need for cash infrequent. Such a policy actually proved a convenience for the cowboy, who had no safe place to keep his money. The system enabled him to save against the time when he might be laid off or want to spend his savings on a spree.

The drought continued through the summer, with increasing damage to the pastures, the severity of which Williamson's letter of August 20 testifies: "I am now camped at the cottonwood grove on Gannon Draw. Moved out from [the] old camp [dugout] on account of the horses, no grass down there. . . . Have had rains on all sides of us but none to amount to anything in [the] Two Buckle pastures."

From there, on September 1, he wrote more genially to two of the Captain's children, Alice and Jud (Levi Jordan): "I am camping out now, sure enough. No dugout, no house or anything except an old cottonwood tree. I thought last night that I'd have to get up and move, was afraid a limb might fall on me. The wind blew terribly, thundered, lightning and raised Cain but no rain. . . . One of my cats got scared and got in bed with me. Only have two cats now, the other two ran off while we were all gone to Kansas City."

On the same date he wrote to the Captain: "Our friends [Two Buckles] haven't begun work yet but am expecting orders to do so daily, or at least they look for CMT [Claude Tilford] daily and expect to go to work as soon as he comes. . . . Will drive all their steers to Kansas and feed them there."

Since the Kentucky Cattle Raising Company had stocked their upper pasture with steers, the prospect of their removal was a pleasing possibility: "If they move out we will have lots of room, won't we? Unless they get cattle to pasture, and don't think they can get them, as the grass is [so] scarce. . . . Well, what do you think? John [Viley] wanted to know of me what you were going to do about your number [of cattle] in here [upper pasture]. My answer was 'I don't think he will do anything'. He says, 'He's over his number now'."

Viley and the Captain were friends and his reference to the number of cattle the Captain was "permitted" to run on Block 28 (740, according to Claude Tilford's comment in a previous conversation) seems to be based on a "law" about which there is neither information nor reason to suspect that such a legal regulation or contractual agreement existed. The Captain was doubtless far above that figure, which seems to have been created by the Tilford's own cal-

44

culations, although it was, it must be admitted, not an unreasonable standard.

Williamson's letter continued: "Cattle are not fattening one bit now, and unless we get rain, and that quick, we won't have another bunch of beef [steers] unless you . . . sell for feeders. Wish you would let me know what you are going to do, that is, if you can at this early date."

When the owners of the Kentucky Cattle Raising Company erected the fence dividing their holdings in half, announced a program of deferred grazing on that portion where the Captain owned no acreage, and instructed him to gather all his cattle into the pasture where they were concentrating their own for the winter, it was concluded that they hoped to eliminate him by starvation. If this was actually a part of the plan, it was certainly conceived with a minimum of appreciation for reality. Range conditions enabling Two Buckle cattle to do well when concentrated in one pasture would also be favorable for SR cattle, and adverse conditions would cause cattle of both brands to suffer alike.

If the central purpose was, as some have concluded, just to create privation for the Captain's cattle, regardless of similar damages to their own, the timing was, in a satanic way, ideal, for, as we have seen from Williamson's reports, a drought was on that would not end until 1894. W. J. Elliot, in his book *The Spurs,* says that the drought was so severe that even prairie dogs died.

We have no record of how many of the Captain's cattle perished in 1891, for no accurate count had been maintained since they were first brought to the Blanco Canyon in 1883. But Williamson's report on calves branded—611 in 1890 and only 160 in 1891—is evidence enough of tremendous losses. His letters also indicate, without giving any significant particulars, that financial difficulties had set in for the Kentuckians. He referred to dishonored checks and indications of herd reductions, admitting, though, that he was receiving hearsay information. At no point did he suggest a Tilford plot to starve the Captain out of Block 28; rather, he ascribed their misfortunes to very poor judgment.

During these first twelve months of residence, Williamson witnessed some basic changes. Probably the greatest was in the relative positions of the competing occupants of Block 28. As previously noted, the Kentucky Cattle Raising Company financed their project by the sale of bonds, the Captain from cash that Duff Green describes as "rusting in a South Texas bank." The Kentuckians had spent their money recklessly, apparently convinced that the remarkably good conditions of ranges, weather, and market prices prevailing when their venture was conceived would continue indefinitely; the Captain had practiced frugality to the point of parsimony. McNeill's financial position, though by comparison inconsiderable, was solid enough to enable him to absorb losses and survive.

No information is available as to just when the Kentucky Cattle Raising Company ran out of cash, or when they began defaulting on bond payments and interest. But in 1891 their financial difficulties were evident, and the process of liquidating livestock was soon under way.

They were not alone in their financial distress. Just one year after they began operations in Crosby County, the Western Land & Livestock Company of Davenport, Iowa, bought land adjoining on the west that took in approximately the south half of Lubbock County.[1] Through the book count and range delivery that hoodwinked other newcomers, they stocked the land with a purported twenty thousand head. Capitalized at $800,000, the source of which is not clear, they too went into decline at about the same time the Kentuckians folded, beginning in 1893, a liquidation process that was not complete until three years later.

Farther to the south, a cattle-raising empire of even greater proportions was victim of similar circumstances within a similar time frame.[2] In 1883, O. J. Wiren put together a ranch that took in most of Kent County and adjoining portions of Stonewall, Scurry, and Fisher counties, stocking this vast area with cattle branded Two Circle Bar. Whatever may have been his initial investment or whatever its origin, during breaks in the market, drought, and blizzards, his borrowings forced him into the hands of creditors, and his cattle kingdom was broken up. In 1901 a part of Wiren's holdings was acquired by J. S. Bilby, who changed the brand to O Bar O. That portion is still owned and operated by Bilby's descendants, using the same brand. A part near Double Mountain was taken over by Hudson and Schultz, two representatives of lenders, who branded

[1] Walter Prescott Webb, ed., *The Handbook of Texas,* (Austin: Texas State Historical Association, 1952), I, 872.
[2] Ibid., II, 297.

46

their cattle Half Circle S. These two eventually purchased the lower pasture of the Two Buckles.

Failure of the Kentucky Cattle Raising Company foretold a period of changes and uncertainties in Blanco Canyon, not all of them pleasant, but generally favorable for the Captain's SR Ranch.

6. Changes in the Canyon

Whatever rumors Williamson had heard about a reduction of the Kentucky Cattle Raising Company's herds were confirmed in general, if not in detail, and by 1893 liquidation was under way. However, no references to this process are found in letters from the SR Ranch in 1892 and 1893. One dated December 8, 1892, addressed to the Captain's eldest son, J. C. McNeill, Jr., describes some events, consummated and planned, that involved operations at the ranch. As a boy of eleven, Jim had visited the place, spending a short visit with his father at the dugout in August, 1887.

The occasion for the letter was Jim's upcoming birthday. He was a freshman at A&M College, and the Captain expressed hopes of seeing him and the rest of his children during the Christmas season. His hopes were dimmed by the absence of George Williamson, who had returned to the coastal region for a vacation among relatives and friends. In his letter, the Captain spoke of a recent sale of steers without mentioning the delivery point, but evidently at some distance: "I had a rough time with my steers, they were running rascals and stampedes were common. I got through with them, however, and sold them for $21 [a good price, in view of market conditions]. Did not lose any on the road, but had to gather them more times than once."

The Captain also wrote of his intention to fence a section of land for a badly needed horse pasture. The location is not mentioned, but the pasture exists today in its original form, two miles north and a half mile east of the dugout on Waddell Draw.

The letter, containing no reference to the Two Buckle, their personnel, or their prospects, was mailed from Pansy, a post office

Capt. J. C. McNeill, Sr., about 1900

had recently been opened on the East Plains some twelve miles from
the dugout. It was located on the mail route connecting Espuela
and Emma, by this time the county seat of Crosby County, and served
as a camp for the mail carrier's overnight use. Apparently moving
the post office from Dockum's store to the Spur Ranch commissary
at Espuela was unsatisfactory to those on the SR. They did not use
the Pansy address for long.

In 1893 the Captain tried a different sales arrangement in the
disposal of his steers. He delivered 394 head to Amarillo buyers
C. J. Miner and William Harral, accepting their note dated May 24,
for $6,113.00, with interest at 10 percent. The deal called for ship-

48

ment to grass in Kansas, the steers to be sold "after they are in shape for market," and the proceeds to be applied to the note, which had been placed with the Captain's bankers, Ball, Hutchings & Company of Galveston. Payments were made October 12, 21, and 23, indicating dates sales were made. Including interest of $132.98 collected, the sale realized for the Captain less than $16 each for his steers, a return foretold when he delivered them and an indication that distress prevailed at the ranch.

However, that same month he shipped forty-six steers to Kansas City that weighed, on the average, 972 pounds, and sold for $2.40 per hundredweight. After deducting freight, commissions, and yardage, these steers averaged $18.86 a head. The difference indicates that the steers sold in May were younger and that their disposal was occasioned by continued drought conditions; the weights on the second shipment give evidence of improved range conditions.

A Williamson letter written in December, 1894, reveals the growing responsibility accorded him, and proves the Captain's original estimate of his potential:

> Enclosed find check for $600. I sold R. L. Stringfellow [early day rancher and merchant at Emma] sixty steers, 3s and up, at $20. I agreed to wait on him for the other six hundred till he shipped them, with the privilege of checking for what little I needed. It will take about two hundred to straighten us out and wind up our affairs. That will leave $400 to you. If you don't need that $400 let me go ahead and build that house, that is, if you still intend to build. I am sure tired of this hole in the ground and lying out with the wagon.

This is the first mention we have of a ranch house, but the subject was evidently not new. Williamson had been courting, mostly by mail, a Brazoria County girl, Mary "Mamie" Reese Cox, daughter of "Judge" C. R. Cox, county official and owner of a ranch down the San Bernard River from the Captain's home. The dugout offered little inducement to a young woman whose environment included a second home in Houston, a beach house at old Quintana, and a retinue of black servants at the ranch home, whose title, Hardscrabble, belied the life-style customary there.

Williamson's desire for a field where horse feed could be raised had been realized. He wrote: "I have an abundance of feed if I can save it all right, which I think I can. Planted something over five acres of Millo mase [milo maize] and it done pretty well. Think I will get fifty or more bushels of grain and near ten tons of fodder with small heads on it. Will begin cutting it next week and if you decide to build up there [the new horse pasture] I won't haul it down here."

He also pressed the Captain to come up and spend part of the winter with him:

> I am getting anxious to see you and if you don't come am afraid I will have to pull up and go to see you. Don't know but what that would suit me best [chance to see his sweetheart?] but will be very glad to see you here.
>
> I am camped at the horse pasture . . . am done cow work except to work the south pasture. . . . Will begin that tomorrow. Will work with the Montgomery wagon.

T. M. Montgomery operated a ranch up Blanco Canyon from Block 28. Most of the Two Buckle cattle had been gathered, but a remnant remained in the lower pasture, and neighbors were participating to recover their strays.

Williamson's poor opinion of Two Buckle management surfaced in sarcasm: "Two Buckles came *near* trading with Halff [cowman in the Midland area]. They asked 10¢ per acre lease and he offered 2½¢. The range bids fair to be all yours for this winter. For my part I'd rather there were some cattle in here besides SRs, as it will be [inconvenient to have them scattered] and besides they [will have to] feed wolves and hungry nesters."

The Kentucky Cattle Raising Company was still selling off their cattle. They contracted to sell a thousand three- and four-year-old steers at $20, these to be selected out of a purported twenty-three hundred. It is doubtful that they produced that many. They entered into liquidation expecting to sell fifteen thousand head, wrote Williamson, but they delivered only thirty-nine hundred after the steers had been taken off.

These stock cattle were sold to White and Swearingen, who had, in 1894, bought the OX ranch in southeastern Childress County.[1] Terms of the deal with the Two Buckle were one-fourth down, the

[1] Walter Prescott Webb, ed., *The Handbook of Texas,* (Austin: Texas State Historical Association, 1952), II, 297.

balance in one and two years without interest. But White refused to make the down payment until all the Two Buckle cattle had been delivered, claiming that they had failed to gather the entire herd. So the work Williamson referred to was evidently part of the effort to collect the remnant of Two Buckle cattle still on the range.

Williamson did not put in writing all his suspicions concerning Two Buckle hands, but he asserted privately his belief that some of their cowpunchers found the management of the company to be easy marks, contriving thereby to market Two Buckle cattle for their own profit. The mavericks created by their carelessness in roundups indicates this clandestine activity.

The close of 1894 marks the end of the Kentucky Cattle Raising Company's Two Buckle brand in Blanco Canyon. The October round-ups in the lower pasture ended their efforts to find cattle for delivery to White and Swearingen. The final tally of their dispersion is not available, but since the bulk of their cattle had already been concentrated in the upper pasture, which yielded only thirty-nine hundred head, the full total must have been pitifully small in comparison with the fifteen thousand the owners had in mind before liquidation. Their projected figure of twenty-three hundred steers raised the preliminary total to only fifty-two hundred head, and the remnant in the lower pasture could not have contributed significantly to the number of which they dreamed.

Disposal of the land was the next step, but success was not easy, and the first significant sale did not occur until 1900 when Hudson and Schultz bought the lower pasture. The actual process by which land sales were conducted is not clear, for the Louisville National Bank in Kentucky handled such transactions.

In the interim the company, or its creditors, sought to ease their losses by taking cattle under pasturage arrangements. Their first confirmed customer was the Carolitos Ranch of Chihuahua, Mexico, who drove to the ranch ten thousand head of two-year-old steers branded Circle Dot, which had been on pasture in the Pecos area.[2] These steers were on the Two Buckle range for two years, during which time they established a lasting reputation for wildness and

---

[2]The Circle Dot brand identified a horse ranch belonging to George M. Noonan that was located on Chacos Creek, in Medina County, forty-five miles west of the San Antonio-Chihuahua road. Frank Collinson, *Life in the Saddle* (Norman: University of Oklahoma Press, 1963), 8–13.

ferocity, proving very troublesome to their neighbors, showing little regard for fences and always proving hard to handle in roundups.

The SR cattle enjoyed the full extent of the upper pasture for these two years. Beginning in 1898, J. B. Snead, who branded Bar O Bar, pastured an unknown number of cattle for two years. Williamson noted that these were mostly stock cattle, that is, cows and calves, although his comments indicate that some steers were included.

Varied and unpredictable circumstances prevailed in Blanco Canyon through the middle nineties, but, general improvement in the cattle business provided an alleviating background. Favorable weather followed the drought of 1892–93, beginning with good rains in the fall of 1894 and extended by beneficial seasons through most of 1898. Steady improvement in cattle prices occurred along with the amelioration of grazing conditions. By 1896 two-year-old steers sold for $20 a head, the same price that three year olds brought in 1894. In 1897 the price of two year olds shot up to $27.50, and old cows, like those Williamson had priced at $13 in 1894, jumped to $22. The market topped out in 1898, with good two-year-old steers selling readily for $28, the best price since 1884.

But on December 10, 1898, a blizzard struck with devastating force, with snow, high winds, and very low temperatures. Cattle drifted badly during the storm, as Williamson related in a letter to the Captain.

> This was certainly a H——— of a spell. For eleven days the creek [White River] froze solid. You can't ride across it anywhere and [there is] never a crack in the ice. Lots of snow on the ground now. . . .
>
> Joe [Ramage] got in today from a week's work in [the] Z Bar L pasture. Our cattle broke the fence in [the] south west corner during the storm and about two thousand from this pasture went into the Z Bar Ls. I missed the cattle off the range and went out there and found [them]. Bar O Bar men riding [the] fence and range all the time reported all OK and never knew anything about the drift. When they found out [about the cattle], their boss wrote Snead that he wished he'd come up here as the cattle were getting out on all sides.
>
> Oh, it is a daisy. There isn't a man in the bunch that knows S——— from high living. I sent Joe over there to help put the cattle back as I was afraid they would chase them too much. . . .
>
> Cattle generally stood the storm pretty well, but there are a good many cows with fall calves that are . . . drawing fast. We haven't seen or heard of any dead SRs [and only] three head of Bar O Bars that

we know of. They don't have a great many stock cattle up here, about 1500, but I think their loss will be pretty heavy . . . as they are poor and a good many [are] old cows.

In spite of the favorable conditions, the north Two Buckle pasture had been overstocked, in line with prevailing practices, and the conditions aggravated by competition for grass. The Captain's herd had increased, according to Duff Green, to about the capacity of the pasture, and with the addition of the Snead cattle, plus the effects of the blizzard, it appeared advisable to move some SR cattle to other ranges. Williamson's letter evidently responded to the Captain's appraisal of the situation: "I will look around for pasture and let you know. I believe if we can get out two or three hundred cows the rest [will] go all right. . . . I think it would pay to move if, as you say, not too far."

He failed to find any of the pasturage desired. On December 20, 1898, he reported that the south Two Buckle pasture was to be stocked with five thousand head, whose owners are not identified but who had obtained an option for a three-year lease on the pasture at 6 cents an acre, subject to sale with a six-month notice to the lessees. Williamson commented: "There has been a bigger rush and grab for grass this fall than I have ever seen. Cattle are so high that owners feel that they must save them."

It was another demonstration of the cycle that has always characterized the cattle business. As had happened before, and would happen again, the cattle market went into a decline, and the Spur Ranch that sold two-year-old steers for $25 in 1899 sold them for $19.40 in 1901.[3] But beyond these market fluctuations and variations in the weather, significant changes were occurring in the late 1890s for the residents on the SR.

7. Farewell to the Dugout

While all these things were taking place, life at the SR Ranch itself was undergoing significant changes. A house was built at the horse

---

[3] W. C. Holden, *The Spur Ranch* (Boston: Christopher Publishing House, 1934), 53.

SR ranch house, built 1894

pasture in 1894 — five rooms with a full basement. Lumber for the structure was hauled from Amarillo, 125 miles away. Then early in 1896 a feminine influence finally arrived, when Williamson brought out the red-haired bride he had married in Brazoria County, the same Mamie Cox he had been courting for over two years.

However radical the change from her father's ranch on the San Bernard, Williamson's bride adjusted quickly to her new surroundings. She and her sister, Frances, had shared the responsibility of nursing their invalid mother and maintaining Judge Cox's household, but the challenge of isolation and the absence of any domestic help must have presented an outright test of her love and loyalty.

Everything indicates that she accepted her new life with neither qualms nor reservations. She typified the strength and character often assigned to women of the frontier, but not always individually ful-

54

filled. This feminine influence was enhanced before the year was out by the arrival of a baby girl, who became the pet of all associated with the ranch. Named Frances for her maternal aunt, she was known familiarly as "Tweets" throughout her life.

If the December blizzard was the outstanding weather event in 1898, the June rainfall was the main feature in 1899. On June 20 Williamson wrote the Captain:

> I know it rained over 12 inches here. . . . Every lake on [the] plains is full . . . and in some places water is still running off the [Cap Rock]. It is safe to say that some lakes in this pasture have 30 feet of water in them. . . . Our friend Scotch Bill [Elliot] declares that a barrel sitting in his yard away from all drainage caught two and a half feet of water at [the] Spur Ranch. . . . There was a three pound tomato can in our poultry yard, it ran over [the] first night. I emptied it and next morning it was running over again. So I can't tell how much it rained as everything ran over but Scotch Bill's Barrel. . . .
>
> Grass is simply fine, cattle getting fat but calf crop short. We will begin branding on [the] 25th and can tell better what [the] shortage is. I rendered 1400 cattle for taxation . . . understand the board of equalization raised them to 2000.

In August he reported branding 607 calves, short of the 800 hoped for.

A Williamson letter written August 28, 1899, mentions the presence of J. C. McNeill, Jr., the Captain's eldest son, who had been sent out as an understudy to his cousin. Jim was an 1896 graduate of A&M College, with a B.S. degree in Civil Engineering. In 1895 he played tackle on the first football team fielded by the Aggies.

After graduation he worked for a time as surveyor for Brazoria County, laying out roads and supervising the clearing of rights-of-way through the dense forests. But engineering was not his choice for a career; he had elected the course, he said, because of its popularity. Moreover, it was apparent that Williamson's tenure at the ranch would not be permanent, since he was not among the Captain's prospective heirs, and that in due time he would probably be moving on to something offering better opportunities.

So Jim McNeill was sent out to work under him, with the prospect of taking over management of the ranch when Williamson should depart. This did not happen until 1902, so Jim had his cousin's guidance for nearly three years. The strong family ties between the Williamsons and the McNeills provided a basis for a closer rela-

55

tionship between the two, one that extended through the years until Williamson's death in 1920.

In October, 1899, Williamson bought fifteen bull calves from R. C. Forbis, ten of which were known to be sired by Hereford bulls and five showing Hereford breeding by their white faces. It is the first evidence of any attempt to improve SR cattle through use of better bulls, a point that had, on occasion, brought forth criticism from cattlemen sharing the range with the Captain. By this time Williamson was evidently accumulating cattle of his own, recording a W as his brand. He wrote that he had added some cows to his little herd and that he would have twenty steers to sell in the spring. He also took advantage of the "free" range situation in the north Two Buckle pasture, taking fifty-one cows belonging to a man named Wilson, from whom he was to get one-third of the calves.

Early in the summer the Captain sent the youngest of his three sons, Keller Reese McNeill, to the ranch in the hopes that the eighteen-year-old boy's health might be improved. The difference between semitropical Brazoria County and the altitude and aridity of the ranch had benefited others, particularly those afflicted with the malaria prevalent in South Texas.

Reese's ailment was apparently never identified. Of him Williamson wrote in his letter on August 28: "Reese, I think, is decidedly better. He hasn't had any fever for over two weeks. . . . He made a hand while branding." But Reese's ailment flared again as they drove a small herd to a Randall County buyer, and Jim, leaving the bunch at Canyon, took him back to the ranch, reporting to the Captain on September 29, 1899: "Reese gave out on the work, so I came in with him. . . . He won't go in when he gets tired . . . think he worked himself down."

His condition did not improve after the return, and it was decided to send him home for medical attention. Jim accompanied him on the trip, made, no doubt, by buggy to the railroad at Colorado City, the usual route of travel between the ranch and the big house on the San Bernard. But home and medication failed to halt the progress of Reese's malady, and he died January 4, 1900.

A national improvement in the cattle business and local improvement in the weather brought a revived interest in grazing land, and, as previously mentioned, the south Two Buckle pasture was sold to Hudson and Schultz. But it is a reasonable assumption that the curious dual ownership of Block 28 handicapped the Louisville National Bank's attempts to sell the north pasture, for the Captain had made it plain that he was not disposed to sell, and the one effort to negotiate a trade with him in 1888 was not productive.

The Tilfords disappeared soon after disposing of their cattle. Thereafter the only name that comes down as an on-the-scene representative of the creditors is that of David Franz, who was also plaintiff in the suit filed after the company defaulted on its bonds. Certainly the Captain held the whip hand in any deals involving sale of the land in Block 28, although his advantage did not extend to control of its use. The situation prevailing over the past seventeen years was warning enough to prospective buyers, and it was imperative for the creditors to effect some kind of settlement that would make the land salable.

No record of negotiations or participants in this final resolution of the stalemate is available, but it is easy to see that the Captain came out well—at least according to his personal evaluations. In a deal consummated in June, 1900, he bought the bank's undivided one-half interest in fifteen odd-numbered sections, plus fourteen complete intervening even-numbered sections,[1] and sold them his undivided one-half interest in eleven odd-numbered sections lying across the north side of Block 28.[2]

The land was valued at $1.55 an acre in both transactions. Thus, with the 8,000 acres purchased in 1882, plus 13,760 acres added, less the 3,520 acres sold, he came out with 18,240 acres, or twenty-eight and a half sections of grazing land. Significantly, the block he acquired lay across Blanco Canyon at its widest part, with an abundance of running water in the springs and draws branching out on each side of White River; four miles of that main stream bisected his land. Less than 15 percent of the tract lay above the Cap Rock, which was in accordance with his preferences, for he showed little interest in its potential as farmland.

Duff Green's self-styled "West Texas Ranch Saga," which was written about 1955 and addressed to Fannie McNeill, is the only written record of the transition period.[3] Although Green's account may

---

[1] Crosby County, Texas, Deed Records, vol. 5, p. 563.
[2] Ibid., vol. 5, p. 541.
[3] Ibid., vol. 6, p. 15.

57

lack accuracy as to dates and personages, it provides the impressions of a participant and the background against which events were acted out:

> About 1900 the Two Buckles sold their south pasture of about one hundred sections to Hudson and Schultz.[4] That left . . . about one hundred sections . . . to be leased, but no takers were found. . . .
>
> That north Two Buckle pasture became a sort of catch-all, that is, everybody in the country had cattle there. I was a CD man, working for Bob Forbis, who had a forty-section pasture on the head of Duck Creek in Dickens County that joined the north Two Buckle pasture on the east, and in the summer of 1897 Forbis put 150 cows [in] . . . with the knowledge of George Williamson, McNeill ranch foreman . . . those cattle staid [sic] there five years, consequently the McNeill chuck wagon wheels were never turned in the north Two Buckle pasture that I was not with them, representing Bob Forbis. . . .
>
> Then in 1901 the Coonley brothers . . . and Julian Bassett, a Crosby County sheep man, relieved the Kentucky Cattle Company of their last West Texas ranch lands . . . the purchase may have been contingent upon the Two Buckle ranch people getting rid of McNeill, or it might be [that] the Coonleys and Bassett bought it thinking they could force McNeill into a settlement.

Green's assumption that the Coonleys and Bassett were involved as principals in the partition of the land is incorrect, for the Louisville bank, representing the creditors of the Kentucky Cattle Raising Company, was the only entity capable of consummating the exchanges effected. Any contingencies Coonleys and Bassett established would have been, of legal necessity, directed toward the bank.[5] They were undoubtedly interested participants in the final arrangements, and their participation probably caused Green to assume that they were principals in the deal.

> All is said to be well that ends well, and one might think that cold and undeclaired [sic] war was nearing its end, which it wasn't. True, the land dispute was over, but nothing had been said about . . . [the] twelve miles of fence [required] to enclose McNeill's lands, so the . . . Bar N Bar Ranch [Coonley Brothers and Bassett, organized as the CB Livestock Company] did the fencing, then enaugerated [sic] a

4 Ibid., vol. 5, pp. 391–95.
5 Ibid., vol. 5, pp. 246–57.

cattle work so McNeill could get his cattle [together]; enough cows for two and a half times the amount of his acres.

Who ever rigged up the terms of the compromise tried to sell Mc-Neill 24 sections of plains land at two dollars an acre [actually, $1.55], which he refused to buy. A man with five thousand (?) cattle on hand and ten Thousand (?) dollars rusting in a South Texas bank vault . . . let the golden apple of opportunity slip out of his hands. . . .

On that Bassett work I again chanced to be there gathering the CD cattle to take back to their home pasture, and saw more burro, jack, donkey and mule displayed than ever rightly belonged to anybody's cow work . . . a sort of 'he fixed me today, but I will fix him tomorrow'. . . . An uncompromising air that rarely gets a fellow any money to buy clothes for the baby.[6]

This may have caused the coolness between Jim McNeill and Julian Bassett that persisted through the years. It did not, however, extend to the Bar N Bar employees, and residents such as the foreman, John McDermett, or longtime hands such as Phil Wilson and Frank Trammel, did their part to maintain a friendly and cooperative relationship with the McNeills and their retinue.

It may be assumed that I didn't think highly of J. C. McNeill. If so, it isn't true. I knew J. C. McNeill, and knew him to be a wonderfully fine personality, though a man of extreme likes and dislikes . . . that was averse to force or compulsion, yet amenable to logic or reason. . . .

There is no question about the Two Buckle Cattle Company trying to freeze McNeill out of his and their range, when he wouldn't sell his land holding to them. They made it rough on him alright, and in turn received about the same treatment they handed out, but McNeill and the Two Buckle Cattle Company's differences was not an isolated trouble between cattle men. Any time a little cowman secured lands in a fenced range and put cattle there, it became like waving a red flag in a mad bull's face to invite trouble that only differed in degree.[7]

The advent of the CB Livestock Company heralded a change of motive in land acquisition, a motive that presented no appeal to Captain McNeill. In purchasing the north Two Buckle pasture and other adjoining lands, the company acquired a large area of level land

---

[6] W. D. Green, "A West Texas Ranch Saga" (Typescript, 1955, in possession of author).
[7] Ibid.

above the Cap Rock. They doubtless foresaw possibilities for farming and acted on that prospect.

Six years later the Swenson interests bought the big Spur Ranch just east of the Two Buckle from the Espuela Land & Cattle Company, which had been operated by an English syndicate with minimal success. They, in turn, began promoting colonization by farmers and cattlemen, a confirmation of the vision motivating Coonleys and Bassett.

As mentioned previously, the Tilfords had a similar idea in 1887, but their attempt was premature. Rational investors could see that large-scale marketing of farmlands would depend on adequate local transportation, meaning, at that time, accessible railroads. Evidently, Captain McNeill never entertained colonizing ideas, although he did consider selling out.

Before the Captain's tract had been fenced and his cattle gathered, he had a prospective buyer. Although his attitude had not been speculative, the Captain wrote asking Williamson's opinion. He received a reply dated September 13, 1900, less than three months after the deeds had been recorded sealing the ownership of Block 28. Williamson responded:

> You want to know what I think of your offer on [the] ranch. Well, you are offered every dollar the market will justify, and I don't see how you could do better if you want to sell. But since you asked for my opinion, here goes: were this mine I would certainly hate to turn it into money. There is no more Blanco Canyon obtainable. I tell you what I'd do were it mine or if I was running it my way. I'd round up every hoof I had, top out 1000 she stuff and sell the rest. I'd then fence the land and get some fine bulls and let them grow to what it [would] carry well and keep it. That way, next year you could . . . sell $40,000 or more of cattle. After this was done it would be one of the prettiest little ranches in Texas, and a wooden man could run it.

Significantly some of Williamson's suggestions appeared in later developments at the ranch.

8. Family Life Develops

In 1900 the feminine influence at the SR Ranch was reinforced yet again. Mamie Cox Williamson's younger sister, Frances, called Fannie, had come for a visit in 1895, returning for another in 1900. Her notes written in preparation for a 1947 talk before a study club in Spur, Texas, give her account of her second visit:

> I had been engaged to J. C. McNeill, Jr. for over a year [and] when talk of going back to Houston came up, my father and his father urged us to be married here instead of making the three-day trip to the railroad [in order to] be married at home.
>
> So J. C. Jr. and I drove to Emma [county seat of Crosby County] and got a license, and the county judge [E. B. Covington] tied the knot, there being no preacher in the county.
>
> For a honeymoon the next day we gathered up the SR cow horses and drove them to the Half Circle S Ranch [formerly the south Two Buckles] where we had arranged to pasture them for the winter, there being loco [weed] in the SR pasture.
>
> And ladies, though I had no shower nor any of the usual festivities. . . . I still remember two gifts: 100 heifer calves from my father-in-law, who had been my friend since babyhood, and $5,000 from my own father, and I felt rich! Our first red-wheeled buggy meant more to me than the Frazer car my husband gave me recently.

For the young couples the ranch house was made into a duplex, and the next two years were happy ones. From childhood the two sisters had shared a particular attachment for each other, and this was for them a renewal of an association broken when Mamie left the San Bernard for Blanco Canyon. Likewise, the comradeship between Jim McNeill and George Williamson had strong roots. The Captain's house was home for the Williamson children, with George accepted as an older brother.

But these were not good years for the ranch. The weather cycle brought drought again, and the cattle market continued to decline. In 1901 Jim reported to his father that they had branded only 220 calves by August and that steer yearlings were selling at $14 to $15 a head.

The human population at the ranch continued to increase, and in November, 1901, Jordan Reese McNeill made his appearance, the

Frances (Fannie) McNeill, about 1900

first-born son of Jim and Fannie McNeill. In order to obtain professional medical attention, the young couple went to Plainview, Hale County, where Dr. Wayland, the pioneer physician for whom Wayland College is named, delivered their child.

Two of the Captain's younger daughters, Ola and Sarah, called Sadie, came out in 1902 for an extended stay at the ranch. When a herd was driven to Portales, New Mexico, the trip provided an opportunity for picking up merchandise not available in places such as Emma and Dickens. Before leaving the ranch, Jim McNeill asked his sisters and his wife what they wanted from Portales. Sadie asked for a barrel of apples, as fresh fruit was not carried by local merchants. But Ola and his wife put in their request for a pair of Mexican burros, knowing that they ran wild in the Pecos valley of New Mexico.

When delivered, the little donkeys provided the women with a new diversion. George Williamson fashioned a cart from a wooden packing box and some old plow wheels, and baby Reese was Fannie's passenger for short rides around the ranch house.

The donkeys had never seen running water before, and when, on the return from Portales, the trail outfit came to White River, they refused to cross. The cowboys' answer to the problem was simple: they roped the burros and dragged them across. In doing so they created a donkey abhorrence for lariat ropes that never faded. Williamson once forgot this and, dragging his rope, loped up to open a gate for the burro-drawn cart and its passengers. At the sight of the loose rope, one of the usually placid donkeys turned the cart over, wrecked the improvised harness, and ran away. No one was hurt, and the congeniality of the group was such that they found the episode amusing.

George and Mamie Williamson left the ranch in 1902, moving to Portales, where they prospered in the cattle business. Williamson eventually organized and managed a bank there. Portales was a rail point to which SR herds had sometimes been driven, and his selection of that locale was evidently based on observations and contacts accumulated on those visits.

The departure of the Williamsons and the McNeill sisters marked a change in Fannie McNeill's life-style. She described the circumstances in her talk before the Spur study club:

I found the greatest lack in my life was the companionship of women, for at times I am sure as much as two months passed with no one about but men.

We got our mail at Emma . . . and we had a box at the post office (soap box in a corner of the room, I mean). The old gentleman who was the postmaster had . . . a taste for literature, and sometimes . . . magazines would be missing, but they always showed up later, minus backs, maybe, for he had some small grandchildren. He was never re-proached or questioned, for reading matter was scarce, and few got more than the weekly county paper.

I was born on a ranch and lived there . . . but ranch life on the coast and here was quite different. There, where Negro help was plen-tiful and reasonable, no one of any means at all did much work. I mean woman's work, which men scorned to do.

The first year I was here cattle were worked four times, branded twice, seven miles of fence put up, and two herds sent [to the rail-road]. That meant from ten to twenty five people to feed, and had they but known it, they were depending on inexperience and igno-rance, but somehow everybody got something to eat . . . at day's end I sometimes wondered if I was afoot or a-horseback.

People lived, mostly, on a meat, bread and potato diet, with canned corn, canned tomatoes and dried fruit. . . . Most ranches brought back a wagon load of groceries when cattle were driven to a point on the railroad. . . . Housewives sent long lists to be shopped for, and most of it she didn't get.

The stores in the small towns got their supplies by freight wagon, and weather conditions were a large factor in that mode of transpor-tation. Such things that happened to merchandise shipped so were sometimes tragic, sometimes amusing. As, for instance, when I sent to a northern poultry farm for White Holland turkeys, and upon ar-rival the two hens had pecked the gobbler to death. Or when the en-tire cargo of flour had a flavor of coal oil [kerosene], or the Irish potatoes were frozen enroute.

Many were the makeshifts we thought up in cooking. I made lemon pies with citric acid and lemon extract that would stump the experts. . . . I gave many people waffles who said they had never tasted them before.

Through her resourcefulness and energy, Fannie McNeill's table became celebrated for variety and flavor, growing out of the plan-tation-type background common to herself and her husband. (Jim McNeill considered any meal that offered less than two meat dishes an admission of poverty.) She developed a knack for preparing hot, hearty meals on short notice, cooking on a wood-burning stove and using kitchenware that today would be considered primitive. Her skill accommodated those who showed up unannounced at meal-times, although the preparation often left her kitchen a disaster area, requiring more time for clean-up than did the cooking.

In 1903 the McNeills bought thirty Hereford bull calves from George Boles of Lubbock for thirty dollars a head. Boles was a pioneer Texas Hereford breeder; he shipped his first registered bull to Amarillo, and, on horseback, led the halter-broken Hereford all the way to Lubbock, a trip requiring several days. It appears that the Captain and his son were following Williamson's recommendations, for in the same year they bought ten Durham (Shorthorn) bulls for the same price.

Following up these purchases in the spring of 1904, Jim McNeill, aided by Duff Green and a cowboy named Joe Ramage, roped, de-horned, and castrated all the Spanish bulls wearing the SR brand. They carried out this reckless performance wherever they found their victims, for there were no pens of consequence on the ranch, and no cattle chute at all until 1922. Their objective was two-fold: to enhance the effectiveness of the young purebred bulls, and to in-crease the value of the rejects, for dehorned "stags" would fatten and command better prices from the packers.

Their standard practice in concluding this operation was to put a rope on the bull's front feet, held taut by a man on horseback, preventing the bull from getting up until another team member could free the hind feet and get to his horse. When given slack, the rope would come off the front feet as the bull struggled to rise, and the team would scatter, usually with a maddened animal bringing up the rear.

Van Leonard, who lived farther up Blanco Canyon, rode up with a companion while the team was completing their alterations on a big bull. Seeing that they were about through, Leonard suggested to his friend that they move off a ways, saying "These winter horses may be a little weak."

Ramage whispered a proposal that they put no rope on the bulls' front feet, and that after the other two got on their horses he would turn the bull loose, run and jump on his horse, and race toward the

SR roundup, 1900. *From left:* Jim McNeill, Duff Green, and Joe Ramage

two visitors, knowing that the bull would be in pursuit. He counted on a laugh when the bystanders found themselves unexpectedly the object of the bull's vengeful intentions.

The prank went as planned until Ramage jumped on his horse, an unpredictable pony named Rastus. When Ramage grabbed him with his spurs, Rastus elected to buck instead of run, resulting in a maximum of motion and a minimum of progress. The bull charged the bucking horse, not the visitors. Fortunately, he had yet to discover he had no horns, and the only evidence of his attack was blood all over the horse's flanks where he had attempted a goring. The joke was on Ramage, and Leonard complimented him, facetiously: "Joe, you sure made a tight ride—man couldn't have driven a knitting needle between the seat of your pants and the saddle."

We have no account of sales made as a consequence of the Captain's settlement with the Louisville National Bank, but they were

66

undoubtedly large in order for him to reduce his herd to his block of land as it was finally put together. These sales were probably made before the market hit its 1903 low, and made in quantity that probably sufficed to finance the additional acreage.

Interior fencing followed the enclosure of the ranch, and a pasture of approximately four sections was created south of the horse pasture. It straddled White River and was known thereafter as the Catfish Pasture, in accordance with the current name for the stream. Another small pasture of about a thousand acres, located north of the horse pasture, was fenced and called Gannon, since it included the draw by that name where Williamson had, on occasion, made his camp under a cottonwood tree. These three pastures separated the main acreage into two parts, designated East Pasture, of about ten sections, and West Pasture, of about twelve.

The first mention of prairie dog control in Jim McNeill's letters occurred in 1903. In that year the ranch fielded its first dog poisoning crew, of which the late "Scandalous John" Selmon, of SMS fame, was an eighteen-year-old member. Dog poisoning became a routine thereafter, repeated as the little rodents repopulated their towns. Extermination did not occur for another twenty-five or thirty years.

Prairie dogs not only ate a lot of grass, but their clearing all the cover that might conceal predators also destroyed larger and valuable bunch grasses. On the other hand, this procedure undoubtedly hindered the intrusion of mesquite brush, for the dogs cut the sprouts as soon as they appeared within their domain. Their burrows tripped many a cow pony, and running a horse in a dog town was to risk a bad fall.

There is no record of an SR trail drive of a length associated with the heyday of herding cattle to distant northern markets. Rail transportation was nearer at the time the ranch began operations. The Texas & Pacific Railroad was operating through Colorado City, Mitchell County, by 1881, and by 1888 the Fort Worth & Denver had reached Amarillo. By 1890 that railroad was serving Estelline, in Hall County, and Quanah, in Hardeman County. These points provided the SR Ranch with a choice of rail service to Kansas City or Chicago, and they were utilized according to circumstances. Colorado City in the 1880s was the only rail point available then; later on, Amarillo, Estelline, and Quanah offered better connections to northern markets and a shorter haul.

Conditions governed choices. Amarillo offered the most direct rail routes, but was ruled out unless rains had been sufficient to provide water in the playa lakes for a drive across the Staked Plains. Drives to Quanah and Estelline offered waterings in the various branches of the Pease River, although problems sometimes arose from gypsum in those streams, particularly in the Turtle Hole area of northeastern Motley County. Sometimes hands were sickened with diarrhea by the water and forced to turn back and return to the ranch. This happened to Jud McNeill, Jim's younger brother, in 1903.

As was noted previously, herds were sometimes driven to Portales. Rail service was available there, but lay at a greater distance from the markets, plus a longer drive from the ranch. It seems reasonable to assume that herds driven there were destined for New Mexico grass and not for midwestern packing plants.

Even after it was seldom used for shipping cattle, the rail point most frequently visited was Colorado City, the oldest town between Weatherford and El Paso. Known as the "Mother of West Texas," it was the most convenient rail point for travel between the ranch and Brazoria County. However, the buggy trip took three days, with overnight stops on the prairie or at friendly ranches along the way.

Jud McNeill, the Captain's fourth child and second son, born in 1880, spent a great deal of time at the ranch in 1903 and 1904, justifying his presence, so far as the ranch was concerned, by his capabilities as a cowhand. If he felt a need for personal justification, he found it in the hunting the area provided. He had developed talents as an outstanding marksman and game getter in the semitropical forests, coastal prairies, and inland waters of Brazoria County. Blanco Canyon presented him with new challenges, and he made the most of them. Pronghorn antelope were plentiful, quail abounded, and prairie chicken and wild turkeys were available.

Coyotes attracted his primary attention, and he developed a technique that engaged his skills as both horseman and huntsman. He trained two SR horses to follow coyotes at full speed in the same way that horses are trained to pursue cattle, and the two he used entered into the sport with a zest matching that of the rider. He would drop his reins and depend on his mount to maintain the chase while he blasted away at the fleeing coyote with a double-barreled shotgun.

On one occasion a chaparral bush broke up a hot pursuit when the horse and Jud made contrary decisions, the horse deciding to go on one side of the bush, Jud making quick plans to go on the other. They parted company, and when Jud stopped rolling, he discovered that the butt of his shotgun was broken off just behind the pistol grip. Relating the incident, he said his first reaction was dismay. But his consternation was short-lived, for through a little experimentation he found that the shotgun was all the more maneuverable with its shortened stock, and his war on the coyotes continued — but with pauses in the gunfire when a bush appeared in the line of pursuit.

9. Places and People

In November, 1903, Jim McNeill bought a small three-section ranch from Handy P. Cole that extended south from the southeast corner of Captain McNeill's SR Ranch. Cole was range boss for the Spur Ranch. He had bought the land in 1897 and built a five-room house where the three forks of Curtis Creek came together, where Pete Slaughter had located his camp in the open-range era. In 1897 Cole recorded Lazy 8 as his brand, but his name still appeared in Spur Ranch records as foreman as late as 1900. He evidently expanded his activities, joining with W. A. Wilkerson in 1906 organizing a bank in Dickens, of which he was elected president, and successfully running for sheriff of Dickens County in 1909. The prospect of these ventures may have prompted him to sell his ranch. The improvements he left there were superior to comparable places in the area, suggesting that his original motives were not speculative. The sale price of the land does not appear in the records available.

It is not known why the McNeills did not move to the Cole place until early in 1904. Perhaps it had something to do with the birth of a second son, Randolph Calvin, on August 31, 1903, again under the care of Dr. Wayland, in Plainview. The boy was named for his two grandfathers.

The Cole house was L-shaped, with three fourteen-by-fourteen-foot rooms in the north to south wing. Another fourteen-by-fourteen-foot room extended to the east, and an eight-by-fourteen-foot entrance hall connected the two wings and provided a passage way from a twenty-eight-foot front porch to a back porch extending along the east side of the north wing. A room about eight by eight was walled in at the north end of the back porch. This was eventually a bathroom after Fannie McNeill managed to get a tub installed there. It was plumbed for drainage only, and hot and cold water had to be carried from the kitchen.

The house was of the "box and strip" type, built to conserve on lumber hauled from Colorado City, a hundred miles away. It included no frame work: one-by-twelve-inch vertical boards formed the walls, with four-inch battens covering the cracks on the outside; it was sealed (when it worked) with wallpaper on the inside. It represented a type of construction frequently used in the milder climates of South and East Texas.

After moving to the Cole place, the Jim McNeills started going to Espuela, the Spur Ranch commissary, to receive their mail. Espuela was located on Duck Creek, some three or four miles west and south from Dickens and about twelve miles from the Cole house. This represented not only a shorter distance than the trip to Emma, but also a big improvement in the terrain traversed. In addition to the extra miles, the trip to Emma involved crossing White River where it flowed through its own steep, rocky gorge, plus, farther on, the abrupt climb up the Cap Rock in getting out of Blanco Canyon. Teams had to have ample opportunity for rest after these tiring efforts.

The trip to Espuela was over a comparatively easy route. After crossing the sandy bed of Curtis Creek and making a sharp pull up the incline on the other side of that valley, the driver of a buggy or wagon entered the West Pasture of the Spur Ranch, with moderate slopes and rolling plains. A good buggy team could travel most of that route at a brisk trot, refreshed by a pause at the Dockum windmill for a drink of water.

Today, few people comprehend the effect that terrain can have on horse-drawn vehicles. Various media attest to the capabilities of horses under saddle, showing that rough country imposes on them no great inhibitions. But horses, in harness and pulling wheeled vehicles, are significantly handicapped by slopes, loose soil, and mud.

The impediment is multiplied when wagons are involved, and intensifies as loads are increased.

The mail came to Espuela from Quanah, the rail point in Hardeman County. From there it was carried by mail hack — mail describing the primary cargo, and hack the type of vehicle involved.

A hack might be described as a heavy-duty buggy, with a boxlike body capped with a rigid canvas top, usually white, and equipped with canvas side curtains that were rolled up and strapped inside the top when weather was agreeable. The box body accommodated two or three removable seats. The mail hack also carried passengers for a small fare, but not at the mad gallop displayed by stagecoaches in the movies, nor was it drawn by four- or six-horse teams. Instead, it was usually pulled by a husky pair at, when the landscape permitted, a sedate but steady trot.

The winter of 1904–1905 was a particularly severe one. Protracted blizzard conditions prevailed most of January, with blowing snow and subzero temperatures. During this month the McNeills' second son, Randolph, was desperately ill with what was diagnosed as pneumonia. His condition was so critical that his father worried about the difficulty of digging a grave in the deeply frozen ground. The boy survived, but never fully overcame the effects of his illness, suspected some years later to have been polio. Although he escaped the full crippling conditions characteristic of that illness, his physical development was impaired to the extent that he never achieved the ability and stamina he might have attained otherwise.

It was a trying time for Fannie McNeill, nursing a very sick one-year-old baby while seven months pregnant with her third son. However, her ordeal seems to have had no bad effect on me, James Calvin McNeill III, born March 27, 1905, the first and only family member born on the ranch.

By this time Dr. Tom Blackwell had taken up residence in Dickens, and was slated to attend my birthing. But hours elapsed as a cowhand rode the fifteen miles to Dickens and the doctor, also on horseback, rode to the ranch. The main event was over when he got there, and he found mother and child doing nicely.

Just how the birth was handled is not clear, but presumably my father and a woman temporarily employed to assist with housework substituted successfully. In later years my mother maintained that Dr. Blackwell's thirty-five dollar bill represented services rendered by merely asking her how she was feeling. Her accusation was a friendly jibe aimed at the young doctor, a family friend from the time of Randolph's illness. In later dealings with the doctor, she accused him of a ten-cent overcharge. He fashioned a clamp in the Dickens blacksmith's shop, secured a dime in its jaws, attached a shipping tag, and sent it to her by parcel post. She kept the trinket for years.

It would appear that her description of experiences as a wife on a small ranch is, in some respects, applicable to the early years on the Cole place, particularly in reference to loneliness and isolation from other women. The house was some seven miles from the SR ranch house and the spouses of any married cowhands who might have been stationed there.

The nearest neighbor lived two miles to the north. Ed Hutson, a Spur Ranch cowboy, had built a half-dugout on a vacancy strip of land between two surveys and had installed his family there. When her boys were quite small, our mother would occasionally walk to the Hutson's place, pulling two tots in a red wagon. Five-year-old Reese was persuaded to ride a stick horse, our mother convincing him that he would not find that type of transportation as tiring as walking. The four-mile round trip included a crossing of Curtis Creek at a point where the valley was steeper than usual.

Some time after the McNeills moved to the Cole place, a bathtub was ordered from a mail-order house for shipment to Plainview, from whence it was to be hauled by a freighter operating into Emma. The order had been placed in early fall. When questioned about delayed delivery, the freighter acknowledged that the tub was in Plainview and that he had given it low priority in making up his loads, feeling that since winter would be arriving soon, a bathtub would not be needed before spring.

As noted previously, merchandise available at Espuela, Dickens, or Emma was strictly limited, so mail order was used to make up for some of the deficiencies. The shortage of toys and playthings for children was virtually total and necessitated complete reliance on Montgomery Ward and Sears Roebuck. The McNeill boys were convinced that Santa Claus was the sole dispenser of playthings at Christmas. So one year, when the presents ordered failed to arrive on time, our mother took advantage of our isolation, swore the hired hand to secrecy, and successfully postponed Christmas until the packages showed up at Espuela and had been smuggled to the ranch. We never knew what she had done until she told us, years later.

In 1907 the SR Ranch became the residence of another of the Captain's children, when his daughter Alice moved with her husband and three small children into the ranch house originally built for George Williamson and his bride. Alice, third child and second daughter, was born in 1878 and married to Thomas Hill Ballowe in 1902. Her senior by fifteen years, Tom Ballowe was a member of another old Brazoria County family and a carpenter by trade. His skill as a woodworker was not well compensated, and his ventures into contracting had also proven unprofitable. These circumstances might lead to the assumption that the Captain set him up in the cattle business as a last resort, but that conclusion is not borne out by any surviving accounts.

The Ballowes had been located at Stanton, in Martin County, over a hundred miles from the ranch. Just what had taken them to this small town is not clear, but is it reasonable to assume that it was Ballowe's vocation. The Captain appears to have disapproved of a trade involving frequent movement and to have offered them a home, a job, and an opportunity where George Williamson and Jim McNeill had made their entries into the cattle business. Undoubtedly, some sort of negotiation must have preceded this journey and its culmination, but again no evidence remains.

Installed at the ranch, the Ballowes acquired a small herd of cattle, adopting a brand called Spanish Y. In time they raised a few horses, among them some outstanding cow ponies. Ballowe made significant additions to the ranch house; he also set up a forge in a small shop north of the house. With an anvil and tools for working iron, he made repairs and created items that would have otherwise been obtained from a blacksmith's shop. In season, he trapped coyotes and lobo wolves, an activity he enjoyed and that produced profit in bounties and fur sales. He raised, but never tamed, a lobo wolf, salvaged as a puppy when the litter was found and the rest destroyed. At night its eerie howling often produced answers testifying to the continued presence of the big wolves in the area de-

Milk house, old headquarters built by Tom Ballowe

spite ranchmen's efforts to exterminate them. When it was nearly grown, he sold it to a zoo in Kansas City.

While these domestic and personal occurrences were taking place, significant developments were also happening in the SR Ranch's cattle business. Fifty-three Hereford heifers were bought from George Boles in September, 1905. These heifers were branded SR on the left hip, a departure from the usual brand location on the left side. Boles received $1,090 for the bunch, a per-head price of over $20.

In time the descendants of these Hereford heifers, bred to Hereford bulls, stocked the East Pasture, and the progeny of the original SR "Orange Blossoms" stocked the West Pasture. They were distinguished by hands on the ranch as Hip Rs and Side Rs.

In 1905 the ranch acquired its first registered bull, a Hereford named Ben D. There is no record of the breeder, but the freight bill

74

of $31.50 indicates that he came from out of the state, possibly Missouri, where many Hereford breeders were concentrated. The purchase price of $300 is impressive considering current markets.

Records of cattle sales are sketchy for this period, but improvement over the depressed prices of 1903 is indicated by the sale of 167 yearling steers for $16 a head in August, 1906. The buyer and point of delivery are not stated in the report to the Captain.

At this point I am compelled to move, an an accelerated pace, from collection to recollection. The volume of available correspondence decreases, and memory becomes more and more the source for relating developments concerning the SR Ranch and the McNeills. To be sure, this story is hereby entrusted to a rather fragile vehicle, where personal experiences and impressions may becloud a more objective chain of events. I can only hope such personal intrusions will not unduly muscle in on the tale.

10. Recollections

Two of the most vivid of my memories occurred in 1908. One is a picture of my Aunt Alice Ballowe standing, weeping, beside the wagon which bore the homemade casket in which they buried her son, Calvin McNeill Ballowe. Born in December, 1905, by accident he got hold of some poison and died in May, 1908. He was buried on a knoll northeast of the Cole house; a small marker bearing his name identifies the location of the grave.

The other recollection testifies to the spirit of my mother. In 1908 my father had surgery in Galveston, where our family was welcomed to the household of Charles P. McNeill, the Captain's younger brother, whom all the kindred called Uncle Charlie. Mother soon returned to the ranch to look after things there, for, in accordance with prevailing medical practices, my father was scheduled for a lengthy convalescence and additional postoperative attention. We boys accompanied her.

This routine was not for my father, and he soon decided, on his own, to leave for home. Calculating the time required for the train ride to Quanah and the hundred-mile trip to Espuela on the mail hack, he wired my mother of his departure and the estimated time of his arrival. The mail hack brought not only the mail, but telegrams as well, for there was no telegraph office nearer than Quanah nor any telephone lines to Espuela or Dickens. How the message got to the ranch I don't recall, but there was evidently delay enough for its delivery to occur the same day my father was due to arrive at Espuela.

Mother was caught completely unprepared. The only team immediately available was a pair of mules named Pete and Tobe. Always resourceful, she hurriedly hitched them to a light buggy. Taking me with her and leaving Reese and Randolph with a woman temporarily employed, she started on the twelve-mile drive to Espuela, torn with anxiety about her husband's condition and hopeful of being on time for his arrival.

The one gate between our house and Espuela was in a narrow valley with steep slopes on either side. When Mother got out to open the gate she took me with her, as she knew the mules were not to be trusted. Demonstrating the validity of her caution, the team promptly ran away with the buggy, bolting straight up the south slope. Mother put me down and took after the runaways on foot, and I can still see her, with ankle-length skirts flying as she and the buggy disappeared over the crest of the ridge. This sudden abandonment in a lonely valley shocked me to the point of panic.

She soon caught the team and drove them back by the same route they had fled along. My next picture is of their reappearance, plunging toward me down that steep slope. It was by no means a reassuring sight, and according to her account of the episode, she had, in the course of events, to pursue two runaways — first the team and then a little boy gone wild with fright.

It all ended well, and when she got me corralled and the team through the open gate she laid the whip on liberally, making the miscreant mules pay for their mischief. Our fast ride across the huge West Pasture of the Spur Ranch took us to Espuela in time to meet the mail hack and welcome my father, little the worse for his peremptory departure and arduous trip.

One other picture from 1908 I still can recall: the location is our kitchen and shows the Captain seated astride a cane-bottomed chair, stripped to the waist, while my parents examined a badly bruised left shoulder. He had been jerked off his horse while leading a bronc through a gate. Because he failed to dally the lead rope around the horn of his saddle, his attempt to hold the bronc cost him his seat, and his shoulder took the full impact when he hit the ground.

His presence on this occasion was his final visit to Crosby County. He never came back and never gave any convincing reasons for staying away.

In the spring of 1909 another telegram found its way to the ranch: Fannie McNeill's father, Judge C. R. Cox, was seriously ill in a Houston hospital, and her presence at his bedside was deemed imperative. Travel arrangements were made overnight, and I recall watching the sun rise as we drove to the gate into the Spur Ranch pasture. We traveled in a white-topped Hess hack behind two good horses, a bay named Puddinfoot and a brown named Billy the Kid.

We headed for Rotan, in Fisher County. A railroad had reached that point, reducing the gap between the ranch and rail service to seventy-five miles instead of the one hundred to Colorado City. We made good time across Dickens County and by early afternoon reached the Salt Fork of the Brazos in Kent County. But instead of its usual winding rivulet, that wide, sandy streambed was covered bank to bank with an ominous surge of muddy, foam-flecked water.

Salt Fork was on a rise, and two men stranded on the far bank illustrated the gravity of the situation. Barefooted and with pant legs rolled up, they were taking a buggy to pieces to extricate it from quicksand. They had gotten the team out and had them tied to a bush beyond the water's edge. It was a formidable prospect, and Father asked Mother if she was willing to try it. Without hesitation, she agreed. We boys got down on the floor of the hack to lessen our chances of being thrown into the water during what promised to be a rough ride.

All it took to get fast action out of that team was a rattle of the whip against the canvas top of the hack. Their response was immediate and slashing, and we hit the water at a high lope. Once in the stream, the plunging of the horses sustained our velocity, and we charged across in a towering splatter of muddy water, profiting, no doubt, by some settling of the quicksand by the previous buggy team.

We soon made it to the O Bar O Ranch, and borrowing a fresh

team there, we drove into Rotan in time to catch the train, but without enough time to arrange for stabling the horses. So Mother and I boarded the train, while my father and two brothers stayed over until the next day. In Houston, we boys were sent to the hospitality of the Captain's Liberty Hall on the San Bernard, where we were joined by our parents when the Judge's condition improved.

On our return to the ranch, I recall spending the night in the Spur Ranch pasture, for the trip home was not marked by the haste involved in the trip out. The next morning we drove into what was to become the town of Spur. At that stage of development it consisted of one frame house and row after row of canvas tents, mobile dwellings for the construction workers building the railroad that was to connect the new town with Stamford in Jones County. The railroad was designated the Stamford & Northwestern, a branch of the Burlington system.

This new town and its rail connection were phases in a colonization program conducted by the Swenson interests following their purchase of the ranch from the Espuela Land & Cattle Company in 1906. The one house belonged to the Mahone family, who operated a dining room for the engineers and supervisors in charge of the construction crews. We had our noon meal there, the first of many enjoyed later in the hotel built and operated by the Mahones. As a child, I had difficulty with the name of their inn; they called it the Western Hotel, a title I felt inappropriate for an establishment on the *east* side of the main street that bisected the town.

For me, 1909 had additional significance, for a cowpuncher and bronc rider named Floyd Wilhoit went to work for the McNeills, an association that lasted, with some intermissions, for many years. During my boyhood I was pampered as his "pardner," an honor I found all the more enjoyable because of his abilities as a rider, roper, and strong man. He enlarged my childish ego by so frequently announcing on my behalf, "That boy's a captain!" that the phrase developed for me a nickname, "Cap," which became my principal identification for the rest of my life.

Early in the summer of 1910 our mother was stricken with a sudden and prostrating illness. By this time Spur had acquired a hospital, built by Dr. T. E. Standifer. When summoned, he came quickly, driving a little early-day Buick roadster. He advised surgery, to be performed as soon as possible. The little automobile, with one narrow, high-perched seat, offered no accommodation for a very sick woman, so she traveled on a cot in the hack, from which the back seat had been removed. The same good team that had prevailed over Salt Fork's floodwaters carried her to Spur at a gallop.

Mother suffered an abdominal hemorrhage that came perilously close to taking her life. Her recovery from surgery was slow, and weeks passed before she returned to the ranch. In her absence, ours was strictly a "batch" establishment. Floyd and our father had responsibility for the entire operation, including the household. The rough diet and unkempt circumstances were not big problems by their masculine standards, but disposing of three small boys was not so easy, and whatever tasks were addressed away from home, we boys were taken along.

Pickup trucks and horse trailers were not yet invented, and even on our relatively small outfit, a trip to the far end was a ten-mile ride, one way. Those who rode off in the morning were usually gone for the rest of the day. As a result, I began range riding at age five, on top of, but not exactly astride, a tall black mare named Nell. Our father treated us with all the consideration available to him, and I recall occasions when I became especially weary, he would take me down from the saddle and lie beside me as I rested in the shade of a bush.

It was a happy day when our mother came home, but her full recovery was slow, and the effects of her sickness persisted for another two years. When, despite medication, she failed to attain the recovery hoped for, Dr. Standifer recommended a change of climate, suggesting that recovery might be hastened by a return to the coastal area with its lower altitude and milder winters. So our father and Floyd resumed their bachelor existence while we spent the winter of 1911–12 in Brazoria County, staying most of the time at the Captain's place. It was an arrangement he liked, for he delighted in a house full of guests and was particularly fond of his daughter-in-law.

Ours was a large room on the first floor, across a wide hall from the Captain's room. Fireplaces heated the old house, and I recall that those in the two rooms mentioned accommodated four-foot logs. On Christmas Eve we boys hung our stockings on the mantel and went to bed full of expectations. We were not disappointed, for in the morning the stockings were full of candy and fruit, with toys and presents on chairs we had placed with care, keeping Santa's convenience in mind. We were especially impressed by a confirmation of Santa's visit, for there in the center of the fireplace, embedded in the ashes, were two deep, man-sized footprints, with other ashy tracks on the hearth. Any doubts we may have entertained about Santa Claus's reality were dispelled by this evidence. They were planted, of course, by our mother using a pair of the Captain's boots, another of her illusions manufactured to support a childish fantasy.

Jim McNeill often found the Captain's criticism of ranch management trying, convinced that his father had lost touch with circumstances and that his criticism might have been avoided or rescinded if he examined the situation on a firsthand basis.

Some obstacles to mutual understanding might be defined here. The Captain chronically overestimated the number of livestock that grasslands in the Crosby County region would support. It was an opinion formed during the years when he had a poorly enumerated herd scattered over a huge range, creating a situation where a realistic ratio of cattle to acres could not be readily calculated. It was a misconception others shared, but they corrected their ideas as time demonstrated the actual grazing potential of this range. But the Captain never fully accepted these limitations, and clung to the opinion that ten acres was sufficient for a cow in Blanco Canyon. Consequently, he was annually disappointed in the size of his calf crops.

Property taxes were another topic of remonstrance in his letters. It may be that he formed a distaste for property taxes when, after the Civil War, the federal government set out to collect back taxes from property owners levied for the four years of secession. His papers contain numerous letters relating to the controversy arising from that assessment and the efforts he and his associates put forth to escape it.

Supplemental feeding in winter was another item that did not fit into his Crosby County experience, and it was kept to a minimum throughout his ownership of the ranch. And, although he had followed George Williamson's advice in 1903 by purchasing Hereford bulls, he was never very enthusiastic about herd improvement.

Although he did not fully fit Duff Green's description of a "typical Texas cow man, that thought a cattle ranch should be managed free of costs," he did like to hold down expenses, as, in 1887, he had advised Henry Tilford to do. George Williamson received $25 a month plus groceries during his twelve years at the ranch. Jim McNeill received the same when he took over, and was still drawing $25 a month when the ranch was divided among heirs in 1930, although he voluntarily surrendered the grocery privilege when he moved to his own place in 1904. This rate of pay did not apply to other hands, for as time went by prevailing practices made advances inevitable. Moreover, Williamson and the Ballowes enjoyed grazing privileges, which Jim McNeill exercised until he acquired his own little ranch.

Final use of the SR chuck wagon occurred in 1909. Cooks were paid $1.25 a day, the high status of that position recognized by the extra 25¢ added to the usual day wage paid to temporary cowboys when herds were driven to railroad shipping points and when round-ups were in order. The advent of local rail facilities did away with cattle drives, and the cooking jobs fell on Fannie McNeill and Alice Ballowe, an added element that would have, in all probability, caused them to endorse the description of early-day ranch life as "Heaven for cattle and men, Hell for horses and women."

In 1912, Jim McNeill purchased twenty registered Hereford cows from the estate of Charles W. Armour at Kansas City. In doing so, he established a registered herd that has been a significant element in McNeill ranch operations up to the present. Armour had built up one of the outstanding Hereford herds in America, supplemented with importations from England, where the breed originated. Upon his death, the cattle were dispersed by his brother, Kirk Armour.

Our father was evidently influenced by his friend George Boles, breeder of the bull calves bought for the SR Ranch in 1903 and the heifers added in 1905. The venture indicated foresight on the part of the younger McNeill, for his acreage (he never referred to his place as a ranch, but as a stock farm) was limited, and purebred cattle represented a way to concentrate his operations by raising cattle of higher value.

However, his decision was not based strictly on dollars and cents, for he displayed throughout his life a love for high-grade, well-bred livestock, an inclination that was, in time, evident all about his home, where cattle, horses, chickens, turkeys, hogs, and even pigeons represented superior breeds and pure bloodlines.

81

He paid $250 a head for his cows, a significant price as compared with current markets and measured against the purchasing power of the dollar then. He accompanied the cattle on the freight train that brought them to Crosbyton, riding in the caboose with the train crew, then took two days to drive them to his ranch. One cow gave birth to a bull calf on the train trip, and Santa Fe was the name that appeared on its registration certificate. He already had a registered bull named Alamo that he bought from Boles. But that sire was, in a couple of years, supplanted by bulls from the first crop of calves dropped by the Armour cows, which had been bred to some of the fine bulls heading the Armour herd.

Meanwhile, other innovations were coming to Jim and Fannie McNeill's small ranch.

11. Progression

In 1909 a Brazoria County relative, Minnie Reese, nicknamed Tootle for no surviving reason, came to our place as governess to begin educating Reese, Randolph, and me. She occupied the east room of our house to be her living quarters by night and our school room by day. She stayed two years, returning to her home for the summer of 1910, then making her final departure in 1911. Her presence was a welcome addition to the family. She gave us close attention and provided the companionship our mother had missed so much after her sister moved to New Mexico.

Our schooling was haphazard during the long South Texas visit of 1911–12. Mother continued the process Minnie had initiated, but circumstances and interruptions prevented meaningful progress until the fall of 1912, when another governess came, a spinster whose brother, E. C. Edmonds, headed one of Spur's two banks.

Miss Edmonds was a kind, congenial woman. We boys soon learned to love her and quickly resumed the progress that had been interrupted for a year. However, she showed little animation or interest beyond her tutorial commitment, and most of her spare time was spent in her room. She acknowledged feelings of languor and listlessness, and made plans to see a physician when she would be visiting relatives during the Christmas holidays.

Whatever our Christmas plans may have been, they had to be discarded, for shortly before that anticipated event, word came that Judge Cox was again in a Houston hospital in grave condition. The notice indicated an urgent attendance by the family. Our departure was expedited, this time by the penetration of rail service to Spur, and after hurried preparations we boarded the train.

The timing of this untoward event impressed my childish sensibilities, for it was apparent that in the course of our two-day train trip, Christmas Eve would find us traveling across Texas in a Pullman car. I was appalled by such a prospect, for I could see no hope of being found by Santa Claus. My disillusionment was painful and indicative of how thoroughly the Santa Claus myth was maintained sixty years ago.

Christopher Randolph Cox was indeed quite ill. We arrived in Houston on Christmas Day, just one day before his death. Always known as Judge, he derived his title from service in Brazoria County government, occupying previous to the office of county judge that of county clerk. Born August 31, 1828, in Bowling Green, Kentucky, he was brought to Texas by his parents as a baby, arriving in Brazoria County on New Year's Day, 1830.

His was an eventful life, representative of Texas in its infancy. Orphaned at age twelve, he was reared by an aunt in Kentucky. After a knife fight, he ran away from a boys' school in Virginia and in 1846 joined the United States Army on its way to invade Mexico. He returned to Brazoria County with a bullet in his leg, a memento of the battle for Mexico City.

He was successful in business, local politics, and in cattle raising on a ranch a few miles down the San Bernard from Liberty Hall. The ranch is now a federal game preserve, still generally known as Hardscrabble, the title he attached to it.

During the Civil War he served as a purchasing agent for the Confederate Army, frequently frustrated when he had to compete with smugglers paying with Union gold, while Confederate paper money was all he had to offer. After the war he served as "Judge Advocate & Treasurer" for Captain McNeill's San Bernard Mounted Rifles.

His wife preceded him in death by eighteen years. Theirs was a large family, all girls except for one boy named for his father, who also preceded him in death.

Our return to the ranch after Judge Cox's death and burial was delayed while the essentials of his estate were negotiated. When we did arrive, we learned from Miss Edmonds's brother that she had left us. Her doctor found her languor to be the result of tuberculosis, and she had left Texas for a more suitable climate. But educational opportunity was still at hand, for an enterprising neighbor, John Zumwalt, had managed to get the county to designate a small common school district, evidently getting our father to assist, as most of the land in the district was ours, and our two families the only residents.

Zumwalt had built the schoolhouse himself, as well as the desks that furnished it, with the county paying for the material. Its construction was the box type used in building the Cole house, but of poorer materials. It measured about twelve by fourteen feet, and, for foundation, rested on four rocks placed at the four corners. Conveniences were minimal. With no well nearby, the teacher and pupils had to carry their own drinking water along with their lunches. A small stove contended with the chill in winter. Trustees Zumwalt and McNeill hauled mesquite wood for fuel; chopping it into suitable lengths was assigned to the boys, seriously handicapped by the failure of either trustee to sharpen the axe.

We began attending the Zumwalt School late in January, 1912, pupils under a teacher we addressed as "Miss Bess," the only part of her name I can recall. The student body numbered seven, including the three of us, two of the Zumwalt girls and their younger brother Jack, plus Chester Carpenter, whose father had settled on a sandy-land farm just over the line in Dickens County.

There were no free public schoolbooks in Texas at that time, so we bought our own at the Red Front Drug Store in Spur. Moreover, given the limited availability, the preferences of local teachers played a significant part in book selection and courses of study, for state designations of suitable texts and grade-level curricula were sketchy. The principal means by which a pupil's grade level could be established was the *Elson's Reader* to which he or she had attained.

The homemade desks were more suitable for adults, and I, the youngest and smallest of the group, found it impossible to read a book lying on the desk top. That level was about even with my eyes if I sat up straight. So I did my reading and studied my lessons with my books in my lap, a practice that my mother blamed for the poor posture that has been mine ever since.

I can recall no critical comment from either of our parents in reference to Miss Bess, but it is entirely possible that we had not been enrolled in the Zumwalt School previously because of their misgivings. At any rate, they took a hand in the teacher selection process before the 1912–13 school term began. It was an opportune time, for Miss Bess had submitted her resignation at the end of the school year. Miss Lizzie Robinson was the woman chosen to take her place, the first of three maiden sisters who would, at one time or another, preside over the little school and leave a lasting impression on the McNeill boys.

Miss Lizzie lived at our house, as did all the teachers who followed her. Even though the pay was small, taxes from the little school district were insufficient to pay the teacher for a full nine months, so our father made up the deficit. None of these teachers was ever charged for room or board, nor required to make any contribution to housework other than the care of the room they occupied. Our mother seemed to enjoy the feminine companionship they afforded her.

So far as the ranch was concerned, 1913 began a three-year period of excellent conditions and improved cattle markets. The SR calf crop was short, doubtless the result of poor conditions during preceding seasons. The SR brand was put on only 256 calves, while the Ballowes branded only 28.

In the years 1913-15, the ranch enjoyed an extremely favorable weather pattern. Range conditions were comparable to those of the late 1870s and early 1880s, when the free-grass men moved in and word got around about the bovine paradise they found here. As token of this auspicious situation, I recall that Curtis Creek, the three-pronged draw on which our house was located, although usually a dry sand bed except when flushed by runoff from hard rains, flowed a steady rivulet of clear spring water the year round. For the only time in my life, that creek was populated with minnows that made their way up from the confluence with White River some six miles downstream, indicating that this flow was not just a local phenomenon.

Under these salubrious conditions, our father began improvements to the place. He built a barn for his registered herd bulls and painted it red. "Uncle Dan" Hogan, a one-armed Irish painter who favored ranch patrons, decorated the long, black roof with signs in big white letters that proclaimed "Majestic Herefords" to anyone approaching from the south, and "Alamo Stock Farm" to those coming from the north.

In 1914 Floyd Wilhoit proudly announced success in his courtship of Ellie Zumwalt. This was no small accomplishment, for the three Zumwalt girls attracted suitors from an area limited only by the restrictions of travel by horseback. Ellie was the belle of the Zumwalt girls, a strapping young woman with a ready smile and an outgoing personality developed against a background of hard work and straitened circumstances. Anticipating the marriage, our father had a one-room house built just west of the ranch house. Measuring sixteen by sixteen feet, it was of frame construction with a porch on the front. Later on, it was to serve as a bunkhouse for hands, replacing the dugout in our backyard.

A large poultry house was built directly north of the new house, with a cupola decorating the roof. A cote for the pigeons was added close by, elevated on posts to prevent invasion by snakes. A little porch extended along each side; built for the convenience of the pigeons, it was soon adopted by marauding horned owls, who found it a handy stage for dragging pigeons out of the nests.

In 1914 we acquired our first automobile, a Model T Ford touring car. It represented our second upward step in family transportation, the first occurring when we graduated from the Hess hack to a surrey. Ours did not have a fringe on the top, but patent leather fenders gave some protection from mud thrown off the wheels and provided a step that made access to the rear seat much easier for women wearing long dresses.

Entrance to the rear seat of the Ford was even easier because it had running boards for steps and doors on each side. Only one door on the passenger side opened to the front seat. The gasoline tank was under the front seat, requiring removal of the cushion when refueling. The car had carbide gas headlamps, and a small, red kerosene lamp served as a taillight. On the approach of darkness, the motorist had to stop to light the lamps.

Registration of these early autos in Texas was a county responsibility and a one-time affair. The owner was assigned a number that indicated the automobile's sequence in cars registered up to that date. No license plate was issued, but the owner was required to have the number permanently painted on the rear of the car. Our Ford was registered in Dickens County as "43."

Neither Fannie McNeill nor Mamie Williamson ever attended college or any of the finishing schools popular among young women of their day. It was an omission occasioned by the ill health of their mother, Mary Cox, that rendered her incapable of functioning as a ranch homemaker. So the two sisters assumed her responsibilities at Hardscrabble, caring for their mother and their youngest sister, Josephine. In appreciation for their devotion and services, Judge Cox awarded them one-half, a quarter each, of his estate. Evidently Mother's share of the Judge's estate financed some of the improvements on the Alamo Stock Farm.

No record remains to show the extent to which this may have occurred, but unquestionably the future of the little ranch looked bright at this point. Heifer calves born to the Armour cows were all retained, expanding that sector of the cow herd, and a ready market for young Hereford bulls was developing locally. The addition of Ellie Wilhoit to the ranch family was a boon to our mother, for she obtained a willing helper and a companion whose assistance was the more appreciated because of the respect and admiration the young bride manifested toward her employer.

Local conditions continued advantageous in 1915, but one very significant development disturbed the course of events for the McNeills: Ellie Wilhoit became pregnant. The gravity of this event can be appreciated only through understanding of the proprieties of the time, when human conception and gestation were hush-hush affairs, however legal. Women achieving this state were supposed to retire from social contacts when the condition could no longer be concealed by corsetry and other artifices. Ellie's situation was complicated by the presence of three young boys with whom she was in daily contact and who, by the same set of standards, were supposed to know little about the processes of motherhood.

A solution to her problem was at hand, for a camp job was available on the Bar N Bar Ranch, and Floyd, highly employable, seized the opportunity to remove his wife from a situation she found embarrassing. Leonard Ryan, a newcomer to the area, took his place. In the absence of the Wilhoits, we boys and Ryan moved into what would thereafter be known as the bunkhouse.

Most of Ryan's previous cowpunching experience had been in Wyoming, and his equipment and performance, reflecting his background, made him a curiosity among Texas waddies. He entertained us in the bunkhouse with harmonica music interspersed with some of the genuine cowboy songs that are now forgotten — sad, interminable ballads such as "Utah Carroll," "California Joe," and "Billy Veniro." These dolorous ditties were appropriate for soothing herds on the bed ground, but I preferred action that was not fatal and characters whose heroism did not result in martyrdom. The songs I remember are "Zebra Dun," relating a confrontation between a pair suitable to the description "a horse that hadn't been rode and a cowboy who hadn't been throwed," and "The Doggone Wheel," wherein a puncher attempted a bicycle after announcing:

> I can ride the wildest bronc that lives in the West,
> I can whip him, I can spur him, let him do his level best.
> I can rope the wildest steer ever wore a Texas brand,
> And in an Indian disagreement I can hold a helping hand!

In the wake of Floyd Wilhoit, acknowledged to be one of the best bronc riders around, Leonard achieved a unique conquest that his predecessor had left incomplete. Two years before this, our father had bought a stallion named Boll Weevil, a striking, high-spirited strawberry roan. The stallion was kept in a box stall, a confinement that offered little opportunity for him to work off any energy.

It was decided that the exercise he needed could be provided by using him to "rustle" (a word never used, in our local parlance, to describe theft) the saddle horses each morning. But when Floyd mounted him the first time, Boll Weevil "broke in two" and went bucking down the slope extending from our barn toward Curtis Creek, putting on an exceptional performance that matched Floyd's ability as a rider.

This digression occurred regularly thereafter, an exercise that Floyd secretly enjoyed. But his employer disapproved, and told him

88

Leonard Ryan on Boll Weevil, 1915

to use his quirt on the horse in hopes that punishment might halt this playful exhibition. It did not work, and Floyd confessed, "Mr. Mack, I can spur him all over, but whip him I just can't do!" After Floyd left, the stallion was used only as a buggy horse.

When Ryan arrived, he used a different approach, setting out to make friends with the horse, and soon the cowboy would enter the stall to be met by the stallion with his right front leg raised. Grasping the leg at the knee, Ryan pumped it up and down a few times in a simulated handshake. Within a few weeks he was riding the stallion with no problems, and in a few months was jumping him, bareback, over feed troughs.

But the wanderlust that had led Ryan all over the West made itself felt once again, and after about a year he left us. The next we heard from him he was in Arizona, and after a ten-year silence, we received a Christmas card mailed from Chicago.

By 1910 Spur and Crosbyton were bustling with activity, and steady streams of new landowners arrived to take possession of their purchases. Some arrived in wagons and buggies, many by rail in "emigrant cars" constructed to accommodate livestock, farm implements, and household furniture, with provision for living quarters to accommodate the owners.

Merchants and tradesmen were quick to take advantage of these new market opportunities, and we boys were impressed with the range of items that became available in the stores — when and if we were fortunate enough to have some money. Spur became our post office address and the place where we did most of our shopping, banking, and visiting. The Presbyterians built the first church there, and our parents were included in its initial membership.

I recall that prior to these new towns, Mother used to order many grocery items from a salesman named J. J. Hammock, who, traveling by buggy, made a round of the ranches at intervals spanning several months. He carried no merchandise with him, and shipment came from Lovern & Brown in Chicago, limiting his offering to other than perishable items. But this gave her the opportunity to enrich her pantry with many things unavailable in Espuela, Dickens, or Emma, such as spices, extracts, and coffee.

Coffee was important. Arbuckle's was the main brand available locally, outstanding for its strength but pungent in flavor. It came in one-pound paper bags and offered the potential of a brew that was, in the words of Bud Leatherwood, "strong enough you could carry it in a sweater pocket."

A pantry had been built in a corner of our kitchen, thin board walls shelved on the inside of the enclosure. The mill was mounted on the outside of this wall and coffee ground in just the amount needed for the meal. In the morning, our father often performed this chore, and with the pantry wall as a sounding board, the racket of the mill and the aroma of freshly ground coffee was signal enough that breakfast would soon be ready.

After the Hutsons departed in 1906, the Zumwalts became our nearest neighbors. They were typical of the people identified as "nesters," those who had drifted into the area with no more possessions than could be accommodated in a covered wagon drawn, usually, by a nondescript team and sometimes leading a milk cow of uncertain pedigree. They were not despised, for they represented a class of newcomers who held few chips in the poker game of life. They originated, for the most part, in settled areas of the state that offered scant opportunities for the landless poor. They made the most of the little vacancy strip they discovered and claimed. Production there was principally designed for home consumption, and they survived through hard work and ingenuity.

The propitious circumstances that blessed this section of Texas attracted attention elsewhere, and Spur ranch lands the Swensons offered found ready buyers. This trend brought in new neighbors for us, and we gained friends whose congeniality served toward forming an informal cooperative that made roundups simpler and more pleasant.

The Putman family established a ranch on the head of Dockum Draw, joining, on the east, the strip that Jim McNeill had bought from Ed Hutson. Their purchase included about fifteen sections, some ten of which had been known as the Tap Pasture of the Spurs. They shipped their cattle in from Marfa, where they had been ranching for a period of years, branding some excellent Hereford cows with a 5, and some of lesser quality with a V Bar. Theirs was a large family, including five boys and two girls. Two of the boys and both of the girls were grown-ups, while three of the boys were about my age. The two older boys, Austin and Bill, were top cowhands and rendered effective assistance in SR roundups.

Just south of the Putmans, Elmer Russell, member of a Motley County ranching family, bought three sections of Swenson land and, leasing another from the same source, put together his own small ranch. His place took in a windmill where W. C. Dockum opened a store in the 1870s for trading with buffalo hunters, where George Williamson picked up his mail in the 1890s, and where the McNeills watered their buggy teams on the way to Espuela or Dickens before Spur was created.

Russell built a house there and moved in with his wife and small daughter. He met his wife in a mode not unusual in ranching country — she had come to Motley County as a schoolteacher and wound up marrying a cowboy.

These were happy times for the McNeills. Our standard of living was mediocre, particularly so by modern comparisons, but our parents were in the prime of life, vigorous, energetic, and optimistic. It was significant to me that they habitually sang at their work, and that their singing was robust and full-throated. I am convinced they sang as an expression of satisfaction with the present and hopes for the future, like meadowlarks on a sunny May morning. Their cheerfulness would serve them well in some tumultous years ahead.

12. Good Times and Bad

For me, 1915 was a banner year, up to a point, for it marked the time when I was more fully embarked on a cowpunching career. Neither of my two older brothers showed much interest in cattle work. For them, horses were just a means of getting from one place to another, and not, as I saw them, fascinating individuals. Randolph was sufficiently handicapped to discourage participation in many activities involved in ranch work, and Reese was by nature more a woodsman than horseman.

I suppose acceptance from cowboys such as Floyd Wilhoit and Leonard Ryan was based on a sharing of interests, for cowboys were my ideals, and their equipment and accomplishments my principal concern. This affinity was not lost on my father, for it fitted in with his own devotion to livestock, and I was encouraged to take part in such functions as my youth and stature would permit.

Thus at age ten, I got my first taste of cutting cattle from the roundup and dragging calves to the branding fire. The SR Ranch had developed some outstanding cutting horses. One that Jud McNeill trained to chase coyotes was a coal black called Nigger Baby, a name that was not, at that time, considered a racial slur.

The initial phase of cutting cattle was simple, as all I had to do was select the animal to be cut out of the herd. The hard part came next, that of staying with the horse while he completed the assignment, something I accomplished by holding on with both hands.

When we rounded the West Pasture, the herd was too large for the one pen available, so the cattle were held in an enclosure next to the pen that included a couple of acres. With that much room, my father let me try my hand at roping calves, cautioning me to stay out of the way of the two ropers charged with supplying the flankers. I am sure the number of calves I dragged up did not present the crew with a surplus, but it was a big day in my life and the second event in what was, for me, a landmark season.

Before 1914 our means of transportation included a surrey, a hack, and a light one-seated buggy, with teams available for any one or all three. I remember the smaller team we used to pull the buggy—named Baldy, a gentle, tractable little bay, and a brown called Rastus, whose instability had been demonstrated to Joe Ramage in 1904.

On occasion, our mother would elect a trip in the buggy, and at some point on the junket Rastus might decide to balk. When that happened she would order us out and with the whip would make the dust fly on the brown pony's rump. Just so much of this was enough, and Rastus would hit the collar running, taking Baldy with him. Mother would take them in a fast circle across the prairie, pick up her three passengers, and resume progress toward our destination.

There was uncertainty in all the teams she drove, for horses are unpredictable and responsive to impulses other than those of the driver. But other than the episode with the burro in 1902, she never lost control.

Curiously, she never learned to drive a car.

It should be apparent by this time that the isolation which had enabled our mother to postpone Christmas was no longer a problem. Even before the arrival of the Putmans and the Russells, we had visitors who came, and, as at Captain McNeill's Liberty Hall, stayed a while. Uncle Charlie and Aunt Ella McNeill frequently came up from Galveston and spent the summer with us, often joined by others from South Texas who found the ranch a great relief from the heat, humidity, and mosquitoes prevailing along the Gulf Coast.

I marvel now at the ease with which they were accommodated

in our house. Perhaps it would be more accurate to say *at* our house, for it is hard to imagine that the numbers we entertained all found places inside that limited structure. I recall that we boys usually bedded down on a porch, front or back, and frequently slept on army cots in the yard, not a bad location in a time when the only air conditioning was natural.

The youngest of the Robinson sisters, Miss Alice, took over the conduct of the Zumwalt School, Miss Lizzie having been called back to a country school in the Brady area.

Originally built on a gravelly ridge south of the Zumwalt home, our school was more than a mile and a half from our house, putting us and our teacher at a distant disadvantage each morning. The school's location was decided on before we were counted as patrons. This inequity was finally resolved when our father and John Zumwalt moved the building to a spot equidistant from the two homes. They removed the beds from two wagons, lengthened the frames with pipe sections for coupling poles, loaded the little house on the vehicle they created, and hauled it across the valley to a point only about a half mile from our house. Thereafter we no longer carried lunches to school except in bad weather, walking home for the noon meal.

In 1915 Ellie Wilhoit presented Floyd with a baby boy, and the complication that caused them to leave no longer existed. With the coming of spring, our separation was ended, and a task awaited Floyd that he was eminently qualified to perform.

The horse population on the SR Ranch had continued to multiply, and by this time the East Pasture was full of stock horses, including a large number of unbroken geldings. After building a round corral specially designed for handling broncs, Tom Ballowe took his family for a long visit to the Captain's Liberty Hall. In their absence, the Wilhoits moved into the SR ranch house.

Towns Taylor, a local cowpuncher and bronc rider, assisted Floyd, and during the summer of 1916 the two broke some sixty SR geldings. Some of these horses were five years old, most were threes and fours, with a few two year olds that were considered well enough developed to begin ranch work. These young horses had never been handled except when branded as yearlings and gelded as twos. As

94

a consequence breaking them was a rowdy, rough-and-tumble affair, requiring strength, skill, and horsemanship of a type acquired by reckless experience.

Pronounced "broke" but not necessarily gentle, most of these young horses were bought by two brothers, Rush and Charles McLaughlin. Sons of farmers in the area who needed individual transportation had, at that time, little access to automobiles, and they provided the McLaughlins with a ready market. Rumor had it that often these young men had opportunity to meditate on the merits of their purchases as they walked home from the places where unscheduled dismounts had occurred, but apparently all of the horses eventually developed into dependable transportation.

The McLaughlins did not take all their purchases in one bunch, and their selections were made on the basis of performances as Floyd or Towns showed each bronc under the saddle. Consequently, of some twenty horses retained, a few chronic bad actors continued testing cowboys on the SR Ranch. I can recall four — Brown Jug, Pet Pony, Light Foot, and Coyote. None of the two year olds was sold, and they developed into good horses — Joker, Cotton Eye, Badger, and Jack Johnson. They were still in use when the ranch was divided among the heirs fourteen years later.

It seems a little odd that an outfit owning so many horses would still buy more, but that was sometimes the case with the McNeills, and occasionally one or two would be added by purchase or, less often, by trade. One such was a little streak-faced bay called Benny, bought from a liveryman at Crosbyton named Seiber.

Our father had given each of us a cow, and the income from annual sales of calves was the major element in our spending money. I took quite a liking to Benny and acquired him by pledging future calf crops toward the $80 cost. I submitted this proposition to the Captain, for the horse was intended for the SR remuda. He approved the deal, and the inflated cattle market enabled me to retire the debt in two years. In 1916 Benny and I won the blue ribbon in the saddle horse class at the Dickens County Fair, indeed a proud moment in my life.

All in all, 1916 was an eventful year for the McNeills and the SR Ranch. A marked improvement in the national economy brought about by the outbreak of World War I extended to the ranching in-

From left: Cap riding Benny, Randolph, and Jim McNeill, 1914

dustry, and cattle markets experienced a strong rising trend. This, coupled with the three previous years of excellent range conditions, set up a wave of optimism that included the entire cattle-raising fraternity.

Earlier gains and prospects for settling the Cox estate presented our parents with the most promising situation they had encountered in sixteen years of marriage. One of the first manifestations of their euphoria was their purchase of a 1916 Cadillac touring car, a make and model in high favor with ranchers. Its increasing prevalence locally indicated the great expectations by which that group was then possessed.

In its day, the car was impressive. It seated seven passengers when the two small seats in the tonneau were used. When not needed, they folded into the back of the front seat. On the minus side, effective shock absorbers had not been developed, and occupants of the rear seat were in danger of being tossed through the top when high speed combined with a big bump produced a vigorous rebound.

Two ranch hands stand out in my recollections of 1916. In the early summer Harold Graves arrived from Brazoria County, sent to the ranch by his brother-in-law, Jud McNeill, to alleviate the malaria with which he was sorely afflicted. A tall man, emaciation accentuated his height, and he did not appear a likely candidate for ranch work. But under the ministrations of Dr. Standifer plus our mother's cooking, he soon showed improvement, and by the time cold weather arrived, exhibited little evidence of the illness that drove him out of South Texas.

Harold found a friend in Floyd Wilhoit and took on such tasks as his physical condition would permit — even breaking a couple of broncs. He made friends with the stallion, Boll Weevil, and rode him regularly. He was good to me, the more so because there was no condescension in his attitude, an aspect that characterized my relationships with Floyd and Leonard. We shared a featherbed in the bunkhouse, protected by the six shooter he always kept under his pillow. This reflected on his life in Brazoria County, where the effects of Reconstruction still lingered fifty years after the Civil War.

Harold stayed with us a full year, and made a top hand when his illness had been overcome. He gained forty pounds and his sallow complexion became ruddy. The pale weakling of 1916 became the robust cowpuncher of 1917. When U.S. participation in the war became imminent, he returned to Brazoria County to enlist in the army. On his return from overseas, he engaged in the cattle business with Jud McNeill. He served as a deputy sheriff in Brazoria County for a number of years and as an inspector for the Texas & Southwestern Cattle Raisers Association.

That fall John Brewer, who had worked as a teamster for our father once before, showed up again and resumed that function. He bunked in the dugout and did his laundry in a Curtis Creek waterhole, asserting that an Indian always washed his clothes in "running water." He claimed to be a member of the "Brewer Tribe." Where? "Springfield, Missouri, or Springfield, Illinios — don't make no difference." His appearance did not bear out his claims: a grizzled, bullet-headed, blue-eyed fellow of average size and definite Anglo lineaments.

He told his employer, in great confidence, that he was a government agent without specifying what type except to emphasize its secrecy, a statement accepted on the same basis as his claims to tribal membership. He was an adequate teamster, a necessary function on the ranch preceding the days of trucks, tractors, and pickups. All the hauling had to be done on wagons, and a trip to Spur and back used up a long day.

When Mr. Brewer (that was the way we addressed him) arrived, he turned his horse loose and never saddled him again until he left us about a year later. When he saddled up to leave, our father told him that since the horse had not been ridden for a year, he might buck, and suggested that a cowboy "top him off." Said Mr. Brewer, in all seriousness, "No, Mr. Mack, I'll walk and lead him until he gets tired, then I'll get on and ride."

And that is the way he left us, walking and leading his horse. We never saw him again, and have no idea what became of him.

In the fall Miss Liza, third of the Misses Robinson, took over the Zumwalt School. The eldest of the three, she was also the most energetic. She did not approve of the tall desks, and no classes were held until, marshalling tools at the ranch, she supervised three of the older boys as they sawed and hammered the furniture into a size appropriate for children.

Our enrollment peaked that year, and the schoolhouse was full with nine pupils. But only two McNeills attended because Reese was enrolled at Kemper Military School in Boonville, Missouri, in deference to the scanty college preparation available at our little country school.

It was a sad parting for me when he left, for despite the difference in our interests, ours had been a very close relationship. We would see very little of him for the next two years, for, because of the war in Europe, cadets in military schools were encouraged to continue their military training in summer camps. This appealed to Reese, and he spent the summers of 1917 and 1918 at camps in Michigan and Illinois.

98

At this time most of the traffic moving between Spur and Crosbyton followed a route passing westward from the West Pasture of the Spur Ranch across the south end of our Alamo Stock Farm, then into the North Cat Pasture of the Half Circle S, where it crossed White River before turning north to enter the SR's West Pasture two miles east of the Cap Rock. The road was not improved nor laned, and passage between ranches was through manually operated gates. Keeping them closed was an unending problem. Public indifference created trouble, as at no point on the route were there people near enough to prevent cattle from straying through gates left ajar.

It had become apparent that Jim McNeill needed a ranch hand to assist him in looking after the Captain's interests. Anticipating the return of the Ballowes from their extended stay in Brazoria County, he decided to improve another facility, including a residence, and establish the Wilhoits there.

The deep, rocky defile carved out by White River through the valley of Blanco Canyon made communication with the west side of the SRs difficult and suggested the desirability of locating a house and pens there. The site selected was close to the gate between the SR and Half Circle S ranches. A barn, connected by a shed to a carriage house, was built there in the fall of 1916, and the Wilhoits took up residence in the barn until a house could be built.

As yet no well had been drilled at the place, and water was dragged, a barrel-full at a time, on a mule-powered "slide" from the south fork of Sandrock Draw, about a quarter of a mile away. But Ellie Wilhoit possessed the background, the stamina, and the optimism for coping with the situation. Still, she could not be criticized for being disturbed when a bucking horse Floyd was riding crashed through the wall of the barn and scattered her cooking utensils all over the room.

The house, when constructed, was of four rooms with virtually no conveniences added. A well was finally drilled, but no provision made for piping water into the house. It was a line camp typical of many located on area ranches and is still known as the SR Camp. Whatever its varied uses may have been through the years, it is doubtful that any one has appreciated the house more than Ellie Wilhoit.

Sandrock Draw

In 1917 our parents decided to enlarge and improve the Cole house. Originally they wanted to add a living room, a bedroom, a bath, and two porches to the front of the house, but when the builder pointed out the amount of loft space that would be added, they decided to develop a second floor with two dormers, using the existing hall as a stairwell.

Carpentry was still a laborious process. With few of the modern woodworking devices or prepared materials now available, the project moved slowly. When the carpenters finally completed their work, Uncle Dan Hogan, previously hired to paint the bull barn, moved in to do the painting and paperhanging. He spent the winter with us, finding the food good and the association pleasant.

On occasion Dan would take off from the job to visit friends, traveling in a carriage described as an "Express Wagon," built with a chassis comparable to a hack. The resemblance stopped with the

SR camp

body, for it was topless, and had only one seat, a high perch at the front of the box. For a team, he owned two small red mules. One was a graduate of a dog-and-pony circus called Molly Bailey after the woman who owned and operated the show. Dan referred to her teammate as "That other damn mule."

They were a feisty pair, and Dan needed help to get them harnessed and hitched to the wagon. Usually, he depended on two men holding them while he climbed to the high seat and braced himself for the dashing exit he correctly anticipated. It was a marvel that he avoided serious trouble and possible injury, but so far as I know, he always made his rounds without notable difficulties.

During World War I Americans were subjected to propaganda on a grand scale, orchestrated in support of the war effort. A special part of that campaign was aimed at agriculture with a slogan "Food

Will Win the War!" Ranchers were urged to maintain their herds no matter the difficulties encountered. Lenders cooperated. Banks and other financial interests specializing in cattle loans offered credit freely, and a general feeling of prosperity permeated the entire beef production process.

In 1916 rainfall was below normal, but its decrease was not drastic enough to excite fears of a drought, and the cattle raisers' current optimism was not diminished. Grass accumulated the three previous years sufficed to maintain cattle in reasonably good condition, and the market held its gains. Rainfall the next year was even more scanty, and range conditions deteriorated throughout. But the call on cattle raisers to produce beef was still urgent, and credit sources continued to provide funds freely. Cowmen, characteristically optimistic, persevered for the most part in spite of mounting indebtedness and bleak pasture conditions.

In the fall of 1917 Jim McNeill sold Lee Bivens seven cars of SR steers to be shipped to Amarillo, held in the pens overnight, and weighed at a price of seven and three-quarters cents a pound. The event stands out in my memory not just because it was the first deal of that kind involving SR cattle, but, more especially, because as a twelve-year-old boy I was present at almost every phase of the transaction and highly impressed with what I saw and heard.

The steers were in the East Pasture, and on the day the sale was made, many of them were grazing on land above the Cap Rock and therefore easily seen. My father took me along in Biven's automobile as we drove around looking at the cattle, while buyer and seller dickered on the price.

Then I was on the drive when we gathered the steers and drove them to Crosbyton. We had no school that year — lacking a teacher — and I found a great deal of pleasure in accompanying my father whenever possible. Floyd Wilhoit, Shorty Kennedy, Pat Denson and Fay Brock joined us on the drive. We penned the steers at Crosbyton, unsaddled our horses at Murry's wagon yard, and spent the night at John K. Fullingim's hotel.

The next morning we loaded the steers and I accompanied my father as we rode to Lubbock in a passenger car attached to the rear end of the train. Arrived at our Potter County destination, we stayed at the Amarillo Hotel, a lodging place favored by cowmen as indicated by the offices opening into the lobby that cattle traders and commission men occupied.

I did not go to the stock pens with my father the next day when the steers were weighed and settlement calculated, but found interesting diversion in riding a streetcar to the fairgrounds. There I hung around the stables and watched the horsemen as they exercised their pacers and trotters, sitting on little racing sulkies with their feet in metal loops so far out on the shafts that they appeared to have the horses in their laps.

My father was bitterly disappointed with the sale. Amarillo was the nearest point where the steers could be weighed, and because of the train trip and the overnight stand without feed, they lost more weight than he had anticipated.

Adding to his frustrations, range conditions became deplorable. Supplemental concentrates such as cotton seed cake were insufficient to replace the lack of good grass for forage. He shipped in hay from as far away as Kansas, with shipping costs added to high prices. Velvet beans, resembling large limas were shipped in from Louisiana; still in the pods, they could be fed on the range.

To make matters worse, early in January, 1918, the area was hit by the worst blizzard I have ever seen. A gale-velocity north wind blew snow into long drifts behind any obstructions, however small. The ground was so bare that soil mixed in with the snow, giving the drifts a light brown color. Temperatures hovered below zero for three days, and on the Plains cattle drifted and died in piles along fences. Fortunately, our range provided sufficient protection to eliminate the drifting, and our losses were limited. But the chickens demonstrated the true severity of the weather — the roosters' combs froze and, after thawing, wasted away.

War and drought produced changes for the McNeills, some good, but most bad. The eventual end of both these episodes left lasting consequences, but with some adjustments life at the SR Ranch continued.

13. Of War, Livestock, and Trains

In 1917 the McNeills acquired a new neighbor when Julian Bassett and the Coonley brothers, doing business as the CB Livestock Company, sold their Bar N Bar ranch to Sidney Webb, who operated out of his ranching base in Palo Pinto County. Soon thereafter Webb offered to buy the Captain's SR Ranch, land and cattle, probably coming nearer to consummating a deal than had any of those who had made offers in the past. His interest in obtaining the SRs is obvious, for, had he succeeded, he would have extended his control of Blanco Canyon from the Crawfish Draw to the south line of Block 28, taking in most of the north Two Buckle pasture put together by the Kentucky Cattle Raising Company.

Surviving correspondence reveals that Webb hoped to finance the deal with the sale of another ranch and was forced to withdraw his offer when that transaction fell apart. But Webb's interest in the SR did not abate, and he approached Jim McNeill in an attempt to buy the cattle and lease the land, thereby reducing the investment required.

This proposition did not appeal to the Captain, and in a letter dated April 14, 1918, he stated his position, with some significant implications: "If Webb can afford to buy my cattle @ $65 per head, and turn in 700 head in addition, [and] pay 50¢ per acre for the pasturage, it looks like I certainly ought to be able to hold the cattle and the ranch for my own purposes. Say to him I am grateful for the message that he wrote you, but that I don't want to sell out yet awhile."

It appears that whatever inclination the Captain might have entertained toward a sale had faded. But his comments suggest that he did not feel that his land was fully utilized. If Webb thought he could stock the pastures with an additional seven hundred head, then the owner should be able to do the same, an indirect renewal of his feeling that his ranch was understocked and that his profits suffered as a consequence.

Permanent occupancy of the SR ranch house ended in 1917 when the Ballowes bought a house in Crosbyton as a solution to the problem of educating their children. Conveniently located for ranching operations, the house was completely shut off from any public school. Terrain and distances were such that even the advent of school buses, years later, would not have provided an answer to the situation.

I recall that the Ballowes had a parrot that adapted to country life so well that it defied capture when they moved away. Calling the dogs seemed to be its sole vocal accomplishment, and thereafter when we drove a bunch of cattle near that ranch house everyone needed to be on the alert, for when the parrot flew over the herd whistling and whooping for the hounds, the cattle were sure to run.

Tom Ballowe and son used the place thereafter as a batch camp, a base from which to look after their livestock and participate in seasonal activities at the SR Ranch.

A normal weather pattern did not return in the spring of 1918, and the normal pattern of life continued to be distorted by the war in Europe. Patriotic fervor remained high, and people cooperated in self-restraint to conserve foods considered vital to the war effort. We had wheatless Mondays and Wednesdays, a real sacrifice in a life-style that counted on home-baked bread as the foodstuff essential to satisfactory existence, rating a housewife's ability as a cook on the quality of the biscuits she baked. Many Texans developed a permanent distaste for corn bread, but discovered that worse things could happen to the staff of life when flour milled from milo maize was offered as a substitute.

Calls for conservation of sugar were enforced by simple scarcity. Local women supported the Red Cross, knitting various items to keep the soldiers warm. Others responded to slogans urging them to "Buy More Bonds" and "Give Till It Hurts" with support from local bankers, who readily loaned money to purchase Liberty Bonds, storing them in their vaults as collateral for the loans.

Reese's absence continued through most of 1918. A member of the graduating class at Kemper, he proceeded immediately to an R.O.T.C. encampment at Fort Sheridan, Illinois, for a month of training. When that ended, he was accepted for officer training under a wartime program designated the Student Army Training Corps, and transferred immediately to an encampment in Michigan. Most of the trainees in the S.A.T.C. came from colleges, and it seems strange that Reese was admitted because he was only sixteen years old. He emerged with the second highest rating in the camp, but was denied a commission when his age came into attention.

Upon his return home, our father immediately escorted Reese to College Station for enrollment in the Texas A&M College. As an 1896 graduate of that school, he was imbued with the loyalty that characterizes Texas Aggies and with pride presented his eldest son as a candidate for matriculation. He was disappointed when A&M turned Reese down, in spite of his scholastic and military record. However, two weeks of the fall semester had already gone by, the school was already overcrowded, and Reese's application was rejected out of hand.

As a consequence, Reese spent the winter at the ranch. He put in more time in the saddle than at any comparable period in his life, ever maintaining a sharp outlook for game. His gear was never complete without a saddle scabbard containing a rifle.

Cattle prices remained fairly high compared with those prevailing before the war, but calf crops were short. In 1917 the SRs branded only 408 calves, although branding was delayed until July. During that work 725 cows were counted, indicating a disastrously low 56 percent producing calves. The average weight of 55 dry cows shipped to Kansas City that year was only 779 pounds.

Nonproduction may have resulted from the lack of supplemental feeds, occasioned by the Captain's opposition to such expenditures. A slight modification of that principle occurred when, after the January blizzard in 1918, two tons of cotton seed cake were bought at a cost of $65 a ton.

As noted, Jim McNeill elected to feed. His choice doubtless took into consideration the quality and value of his cattle, for he had saved all the heifers produced by the Armour cows, thereby increasing his registered herd. Moreover, he had improved the descendants of the heifers given by the Captain as a wedding gift in 1900 to the extent that he was by this time selling most of the bull calves for breeding stock.

A penciled memorandum dated October 4, 1918, indicates his progress:

James McNeill to Swenson Bros.
    Approximately 25 Registered bull calves born before June 1st,
1918, and including approximately 10 born before Jan. 1st, 1918.
Approximately 25 head of same ages either out of Registered Here-

106

ford cows or unregistered Hereford cows with [a] small undercurrent [of] full blood Shorthorn, and all by Registered Hereford bulls at $100 a head.

Also one 2 year old Registered bull at $400, and one Registered yearling bull at $500.

All for delivery at [the] old headquarters, Spur [Ranch], Oct. 9, 1918. One thousand dollars cash is hereby paid and acknowledged. Balance to be placed to acct. of James McNeill, Spur National Bank, upon advice of delivery.

Signed:

J. C. McNeill

Swenson Bros.
F. S. Hastings, Mgr.

The stock horses running in the East Pasture presented a problem that had been growing as the herd multiplied. The situation was not unique with the SRs, for other ranches in the area were experiencing similar difficulties, and the underlying causes were generally the same: a lack of demand for mares. They were considered useful for breeding purposes only, and the ranches raising their own saddle horses already had, in most instances, more mares than they needed.

Under these circumstances, the SR horse herd had steadily multiplied until it was seriously limiting the number of cattle the pasture could support. As far back as March, 1913, the Captain had commented in a letter, "I believe your idea about selling all the female SR horses a good one. They undoubtedly eat more grass than cows, and there are too many of them." An undated entry in that year's cash accounts shows that fifteen mares were sold to Murry & Seiber for $65 a head, the only sale of mares recorded.

Jim McNeill observed the adverse probabilities of these stock horses early in his tenure as ranch manager. A draft-type stallion was bought in 1915 for $350, and in 1916 thirty-three big-hipped colts were branded. But the market outlook for these prospective plow horses was dismal, and in 1918 he sold the entire herd, numbering, besides colts, about one hundred twenty-five mares, two year olds, and yearlings. The buyer was a man from Oklahoma, and the price a flat $3,000. The Captain's reaction to the sale, dated April 16, 1918: "Your letter and check to hand. Yes, you gave the horse stock away, but I am glad they are off the range."

In the same year a neighboring ranch sold several carloads of range mares for $3.50 a head. The buyer apparently experienced early regrets and overloaded the cars in hopes that many would be trampled to death, enabling him to collect a portion of his investment from the railroad.

In February, 1919, the Wilhoits left the SR Ranch, never to return as employees. Compared with cowboys of similar skills as horseman, roper, and range hand, Floyd was unique in that he willingly took on jobs that many punchers of his caliber shunned, perferring to limit their activities to "anything that can be done a-horseback." A powerful man, he seemed to derive pleasure in tasks requiring strength and stamina. He built several miles of fences on the ranch at a time when motor-driven hole diggers had yet to be invented. Opportunities beckoned in Eastland and Stephens counties, where booming oil fields had sprung up. All drayage there was by wagon and team over unpaved roads, and Floyd had secured the backing for mules and equipment to outfit several units.

Personally, I was devastated by their departure, for they were a part of my life. As my father's means of communication with the SR Camp, I often made the ride with pleasure, for it usually included an overnight stay with the Wilhoits: Floyd, Ellie, and their son, Buck. As a remembrance after they left, I proudly wore Floyd's jangling spurs, probably the noisiest ever made by the famous blacksmith, J. O. Bass, of Tulia, Texas.

McNeill bulls were in demand, particularly in Motley and Floyd counties, where a number of smaller ranches were located in an area dominated by the huge Matador Ranch. In the spring of 1922 a small group of these cattlemen came to look at bulls and were caught in a hard rain after they arrived. Curtis Creek became a torrent, temporarily preventing their return, so they spent the night.

For them, and my father, it was a jolly reunion, and they whiled away the hours on our front porch, playing dominoes and swapping yarns. The group included A. B. Echols and his son Bob, L. H. "Lal" Lewis, Ed Lisenby, and Quin Clutts.

An entranced audience of one, I recall a particular segment of their conversation that impressed me with its humor and references to incidents that happened while shipping cattle to market. Caretakers accompanying the cattle were provided with tickets for their return by passenger train, and the conversation dealt with things that happened on some of those return trips. Here are a couple:

Two Motley County cowmen, nameless here, boarded a train, and when the porter came through announcing "Dining car in the rear," decided to try this unexpected convenience. Seated there, they paid little attention to menu, for they knew what they wanted: steak and potatoes, hot bread, pie and coffee, so that was their order.

When the check was presented, they were outraged, objected strenuously, and demanded to see the dining car conductor. He sought to explain the charges, pointing out the convenience and the elegance of the surroundings, and indicating, in this connection, the linen drapery and the rose on the table in its cut glass vase.

"Do you mean," demanded one of the cowmen, "that we have to pay for that flower too?"

"Well," the conductor replied, "it has to be figured in with all the things we are providing for the comfort of our passengers."

The cowman shook a threatening finger under the conductor's nose and growled, "Son, if we are paying for it, ain't nobody else gonna smell it!"

And seizing the vase, he hurled it out the window. The check was quickly refigured to include the cost of the vase and the screen that accompanied it in its ejection.

Another cowman, also nameless here, tarried at the stockyards before leaving to catch his train. On the way to the station he stopped at a shoe store, for his boots were old and down at heel, and wading through the mucky pens had rendered them socially unacceptable.

He told the clerk what he wanted and specified the size. The clerk selected a box, pulled out a shoe, and made ready to try it on the customer. The cowman demurred, "That's just what I want, and I don't have time to try them on, for I'm hurrying to catch a train."

He paid the clerk and made it to the station just in time to get aboard. Settled in his seat, he decided to discard his dilapidated, odorous boots, and pulling a shoe from the box, took off the corresponding boot and, raising the screen, tossed it out the window. When he had laced the shoe, he pulled off the other boot and, after it went out the window, took the other shoe from the box.

The two shoes were for the same foot.

Making his contribution, my father said he was returning from Kansas City in company with some men from the Amarillo area.

As they boarded, the conductor, as usual, asked each to name his destination:

"Quitaque," answered a man from Briscoe County,[1] using the local pronunciation, which sounded like "Kitty Kway."

"What?" asked the conductor.

"Quitaque," the man reiterated.

The conductor looked puzzled. "Would you please spell it?" he asked.

"Aw, just let it go," said the cowman, "I've decided to get off at Plainview."

These significant anecdotes pertain to a feature of marketing cattle — railroad transportation — that lasted locally for at least fifty years. We usually shipped from Crosbyton, for routings were better from that point. It was, moreover, an easier drive than to Spur, as the north west corner of the SR was only three miles from the Crosbyton stock pens.

During the 1920s the Santa Fe Railroad instituted a special train for cattle shipments only, originating near Houston and picking up consignments until becoming a through train at Amarillo. It reached Lubbock Friday afternoon each week. The mixed train that left Crosbyton by eight o'clock made connection at Lubbock, and the cattle were unloaded in Kansas City in time to be fed, watered, and ready for sale on Monday.

Such special service indicates that the railroads wanted the business, but that inclination was seldom reflected among their operating employees, who were almost uniformly hostile and uncooperative. At times this animosity was vented on the cattle with jolting stops and sudden starts that caused unnecessary crowding and, for animals that fell, trampling that was often crippling and sometimes fatal.

In a letter dated October 27, 1914, reporting sales at Kansas City, Jim McNeill wrote the Captain: "Shipped 95 head of cattle for you, five were killed at Waynoka (Kansas) by mad engineer."

[1] "How the name Quitaque was applied to that range is an interesting bit of frontier history. Once when General Mackenzie and his famous cavalry raiders were chasing Bull Bear and his band of Antelope Apaches, the wily Indian chief used a clever ruse to throw Mackenzie off his trail. The Indians were driving hundreds of horses. Bull Bear had his braves gather batches of fresh horse manure and strew it in the opposite direction to their escape route. The ruse not only worked but gave a name to that part of the High Plains." Frank Collinson, *Life in the Saddle* (Norman: University of Oklahoma Press, 1963), 58.

Other letters and ranch records refer to similar incidents and injuries. Of course, in those instances claims were filed, sometimes paid, sometimes contested, but always at a net loss to the shipper. An entry in 1921 records that a refund of $541.66 was paid on a claim filed in 1918—eighteen months after the injuries occurred.

My cowpunching days started too late to experience drives to Amarillo or Estelline, and my father would never make any claims to "going up the trail," holding that the drives he made were not long enough to qualify for that distinction. He said, however, that most of what he knew about trailing cattle he learned from Duff Green and cited an instance of that adviser's sagacity.

He said they had started to Portales with a herd and had camped just west of the village called Lubbock. He estimated their campsite at about the present location of Texas Tech. The night proved to be particularly dark, and Green advised him to pick up the hands taking the first stand on guard as quietly as possible and have the entire crew crawl into their hot rolls and go to sleep. Green explained: "Riders wandering around in this darkness are apt to get among the cattle and start them running, and you will do better to just stay away from them."

Early the next morning the cattle were up and grazing, but still close by. After gathering them and cutting out a few strays, the outfit proceeded on its way in good form.

The principal buyer of SR calves in the 1920s was R. C. "Bob" Forbis. He had an associate named Parrett located in the Corn Belt where most of the pen-fed cattle were developed for market. Essentially, their arrangement was based on Forbis as the buyer in the area where the calves were produced and Parrett as the seller in the area to which they were shipped.

In the fall, delivering the calves to a shipping point was tricky business. It involved cutting them from their mothers and driving them to the railroad. Herding newly separated young calves was a ticklish assignment, and I recall a situation on the Putman ranch that ended in disaster.

We had spent two days gathering their cattle and concentrating the calves in pens after separation from the cows. Several new faces were included in the crew assembled the third morning, as the Putmans anticipated trouble. Before the gates were opened, several men were tightening cinches and getting ropes ready for quick usage. It was a harbinger of failure, my father cautioned me in an aside, pointing out that any time one of these cowboys roped a calf his usefulness for herd control would be lost.

Matador was the shipping point set up by the buyers. The route of the drive lay across the headquarters division of the SMS Ranch, which adjoined the Putmans on the east. As expected, the calves came out running, but were easily pointed in the proper direction. Surrounded on three sides by horsemen, they ran closely bunched for a half a mile, when some began to slow down, and soon we had calves traveling at various speeds in a formation two hundred yards long. The intervals between riders increased as the herd lengthened.

And this led to trouble, for soon a calf near the middle of the line turned off, dodged behind a cowboy, and headed away from his fellows. The cowboy pursued, swinging his rope, and in minutes other calves and other riders were doing the same thing. In another ten minutes the herd had disintegrated, with calves scattering and turning back toward their home range.

We lost all but a handful. The rest went back to their mothers, and all we could do was to take the laggards and start all over, spending the next two days working the pastures and penning the calves once more. Bill Putman appealed to my father for advice, and following his instructions, delivered the calves to the Matador stock pens three days later than scheduled.

Jim McNeill's method was simple: he made sure that all the calves ran at the same pace, which would be set by those most disposed to run, and forcing the rest to keep up with them. By doing so the initial compact formation would be maintained, and riders kept close together.

When we delivered SR calves, he never took a position at the side of the herd, but at the rear with the "drag," generally regarded as an inferior position. But his performance there was something else. Sometimes he would arm himself with a gallon can containing a few rocks, and the racket he created with this rattle would make sluggish calves run with the wilder ones. He could produce the same effect wielding a slicker (raincoat), waving it overhead and slapping stragglers to keep them running.

The result of his performance and the example he set served to keep the calves together until they were all ready to slow down to a walk. We never had any trouble driving calves off in the fall.

The end of World War I, November 11, 1918, was a day of jubilation in the cities, towns, and villages of America, but the McNeills did not know about it until two days later. Our principal source of national news — the Fort Worth *Star-Telegram* — brought us up to date only when someone went to the post office.

The wartime euphoria that had been maintained through drought and indebtedness would, for cattlemen, gradually evaporate in a new and more realistic atmosphere.

14. The Postwar Years

In the winter of 1918–19 residency on the McNeill ranches was limited to the family, including Reese after his rejection by Texas A&M, plus ranch hand Steve Keith and a black cook named Stella, imported by Uncle Charlie and Aunt Ella when they came for a summer-long visit. The SR ranch house was vacant as was the Zumwalt School, lacking a teacher.

When the influenza epidemic struck that year, all at our house were stricken except Reese and myself. We divided our responsibilities so that I looked after the cattle while he attended the sick. Our father was the most seriously ill, developing pneumonia. He survived the ordeal, but his recovery was slow and months passed before he regained his normal capabilities.

In the spring of 1919 he bought his first tractor, an Illinois Super-Drive. It was an early indication that he believed survival as a small rancher must involve more cultivated land. Ed Hutson had broken out thirty acres north of his half-dugout, and when our father bought that strip from him, he added thirty adjoining cultivated acres. These two fields were regularly planted to milo maize or kindred sorghums that supplied us with grain for horses, milk cows, and hogs, while Johnson grass raised on a small field near the ranch house was mowed, raked, and hauled in for fodder.

A few years later, approximately a hundred acres of the Hutson strip that lay above the Cap Rock was put into cultivation, the best farming land on the place but, at the time, inconveniently located. The new tractor indicated our father's aspirations, but it preceded later inventions adapted for working row crops, and his limited plowland acres did not fully realize their potential.

When, in 1918, the SR Ranch sold all its brood mares, horse breeding was not completely eliminated, for our father still owned a small band kept in the two-section pasture north of our house. They were no gentler than the SR band that had been sold for a song, but were, through superior breeding, speedier. They were a nuisance to handle, and no one was available to break the geldings.

My father decided to sell the mares, and found a buyer in Doc Husky, a horse-trading veterinary at Floydada. In June, 1920, Husky came with his two teenaged boys, Osie and Dallas, proposing to take all the mares remaining and any disposable unbroken geldings. A Floyd County barber, whose name I do not recall, came with them, seizing this opportunity for a return to cowboying. My father hired a cook named Albin, and we moved into the vacant SR Camp. We put in a hard week there, alternating the work by branding calves one day, with help from the Putmans, and running wild horses the next.

We had an outlaw — a slim black gelding about four years old — that had gotten into the Catfish Pasture, where he subsisted alone as wild as a bird. Although that pasture enclosed only about four sections, it was a particularly rough area. White River made its canyon throughout its length, intersected on the east by two branch canyons called China Hollow and Horse Pasture Draw. Sand Rock Draw entered from the west in a still more formidable chasm.

Three of us — my father, Boney Fields, and I — had made two attempts the previous week to get the black pony out of that pasture. Both ventures failed as the outlaw sailed down declivities where we dared not follow, using the time gained to hide in the brush along the river.

With a larger crew available, we set out to bring him in. We drove our entire saddle band into the west side of the pasture, where a couple of riders herded them as they grazed. The rest of us spread out, and when the black was found, passed him from one to another in a quick succession that gave him no opportunity to hide.

As planned, he soon joined the saddle band, and we started back to the camp, feeling that we finally had him under control.

But as we crossed a corner of the twelve-section West Pasture, and before we could drive the bunch through the second gate, the outlaw quit the saddle horses, and, heading north, outran his pursuers. He was finally brought back, after making a tour of the larger area, with relays of riders chasing him for a fast nine or ten miles.

When we had him penned at the camp with the other horses, my father had him roped and thrown down. He then tied a half-inch iron nut in the horse's fore-top, that portion of the mane extending beyond the ears. This was supposed to be a proven annoyance causing the horse to shake his head and produce a self-inflicted thumping that would soon discourage any excessive movement, including, hopefully, running.

The black stayed with the bunch until we got into the pasture north of our house. There he suddenly departed again, carrying his head at a protective angle with the iron nut cocked behind one ear. He headed for the steep bluffs and rocky outcroppings along Curtis Creek.

In the chase that ensued, the barber/cowboy from Floydada cornered the runaway against the clay banks of a U-shaped bend in the draw so that the escapee had to come out within roping range. But the black's entire head did not go through the cowboy's loop, and by sheer luck the noose drew up on the nut and held there. Amazement prevailed when the cowboy came back to the saddle horses, slowly and carefully leading the outlaw by the little patch of hair on the top of his head.

I never knew how Husky came out on his purchases, but I often wondered about the black gelding, who had demonstrated speed and stamina, plus, in a pinch, an unusual amount of intelligence.

There was never another mare in the McNeill's pastures for the next sixty years.

The economic recession beginning in 1920 became a depression as the nation went through severe postwar deflation. Cattle prices declined in 1920 and plummeted in 1921. In May, 157 steer calves carried over from the preceding year sold in Kansas City for an average of $7.25 per hundredweight. In November, 319 steer calves sold on the same market for an average of only $4.92 per hundredweight and, because of their lighter weight, that should have been a premium price. The Captain wrote of the situation in Brazoria County: "Cattle have slumped in price here . . . until buyers are afraid to buy and banks skeptical over securities."

Actually, the cattle market was the lesser of his problems, for sorrow had invaded his house when, in May, 1919, Sadie died in a Galveston hospital. She had performed with energy and good will as the Captain's housekeeper, supervising several black servants and dispensing hospitality to the many and varied visitors. She was only thirty-six years old, and unmarried. Then in 1921, death claimed another member of the Captain's family. His youngest daughter, Ann, died in childbirth. Married to Oscar Olsen in 1914, she had made her home a short distance from the Captain's house. Her child died as well.

If this was not enough, disaster continued on the San Bernard that year when Liberty Hall burned to the ground. Built in the early 1850s by the Mims family, colonists under Stephen F. Austin, most of its contents were recovered, but the house itself was a total loss.

The family set up housekeeping in a big, red barn left untouched by the flames. Following Sadie's death, Liberty Hall acquired a new chatelaine. Jud McNeill had married Sarah Graves in 1909, and they moved in with their two children, Little Sarah (her name from then on) and L. J. McNeill Jr.

"Miss Sarah" took over the arduous responsibilities of the lifestyle so firmly established in the Captain's household, coping with the problems of housekeeper and hostess. The Captain still loved to have guests and habitually brought in relatives and acquaintances on short notice.

Temporary residence in the barn did not curb his hospitality, creating new problems for his daughter-in-law. Given her notions of decorum, she found the lack of privacy a disconcerting handicap. When late one afternoon the Captain brought home some men with whom she had no previous acquaintance, the gracious lady gathered up her night clothes and departed, exclaiming, "I've slept with my in-laws, and I've slept with my out-laws, but I draw the line at sleeping with strange men!" She spent the night at her mother's home in Brazoria.

Fortunately, the Captain had in his household a capable builder in Jud McNeill, and rebuilding was quickly set in motion. Jud planned the new house, selected the materials, and supervised the construction, developing a house designed to withstand the hurricanes endemic to the Gulf Coast.

After the Wilhoits left, Guy Merriman moved into the SR Camp. Young and single, the solitude was too much for him, and he lasted less than five months. Handicapped by his departure, Jim McNeill wrote the Captain in 1920: "Men are scarce and they want 5 dollars a day and board, or $50 or $60 a month, and the good ones are not to be had. I have more than I can do."

In July he capitulated to conditions and hired A. V. Hays at $75 a month. This Matador cowboy disliked any work that had to be done afoot and was "let out" in the fall. His main accomplishment was the conversion of some SR horses to accommodate his left-handed technique as he practiced roping on SR cattle.

Lon Holleymon moved his family into the camp in April, 1921. For years a top hand on John Slaughter's ranch in eastern New Mexico, he got into the cattle business on borrowed capital in the boom years, went broke in the drought of 1916-18, and took refuge in the Texas oil fields. When that activity slowed down he came to Spur and took a job feeding cattle at the Texas Agricultural Experiment Station. On the recommendation of R.E. Dickson, superintendent, Jim McNeill gave him the job.

Lon's performance on the SR Ranch was outstanding. The place had always lacked adequate cattle pens, and Lon corrected this at the SR Camp with a well-built pattern that facilitated handling cattle in ways not possible before. He maintained a close watch on the cattle, riding at a swinging trot, always standing erect in his stirrups. We developed a saying among ourselves: "If you want to see Lon, just ride up on a hill somewhere, and he will be along in a few minutes." He rode a number of SR horses, but seldom a fat one, for they lacked the leisure to put on extra weight.

Lon's ability as a cowhand was enhanced by his popularity. He was witty and outgoing and possessed a knack for relating his experiences and observations in a style his comtemporaries appreciated. He improved the morale of any group with which he worked. As an employee Lon had only one weakness, for he was accident prone, often disregarding his personal safety when a critical situation indicated quick action. On occasion he was incapacitated for days, though never during this term of employment was he permanently injured.

The slump in cattle prices produced an even greater break in Jim McNeill's bull sales. Some buyers demanded, and got, lower bull prices, but most simply quit buying, deferring replacements and planned herd improvements. His herd of young bulls became a burdensome accumulation, and it was a welcome event when his neighbor, Frank Corn, came with his ranch manager, Zay Powell, looking for bulls.

Corn, who lived in Fort Worth, ranched over an area of about a hundred fifty sections, including the one-time lower pasture of the Two Buckles, bought from A. W. Hudson in 1915, to which he had added the Z Bar L range. The precise number of bulls he bought is not recorded, but it was the largest since Frank Hastings's purchase of fifty-two head in 1918 and occurred at a critical time. Corn asked for ninety days delay in payment, which was granted, and insisted on giving his note for the amount, which was accepted, contrary to practices current at the time.

However, the note was not paid when due, and soon thereafter Corn filed in bankruptcy, an action that shocked area cowmen. Since no lien was attached to the note, the bulls were claimed by secured creditors. This aggravated our father's financial problems, for he had gone deeply in debt to care for his cattle and preserve their numbers through the drought and the severe weather that accompanied it.

The euphoria generated by the wartime boom in cattle prices brought about the creation of companies specializing in cattle loans. Such a group developed at Spur under the title Spur Cattle Loan Company with Clifford B. Jones, resident manager of the Swenson land sales program, as president. When depression hit the cattle business, these lenders lost their enthusiasm. No longer did they solicit loans, but applied their efforts toward liquidating those already outstanding. This put many debt-ridden cattlemen in a bind, with no source of funds for operations other than borrowing on their lands. Many who could not qualify simply went out of business, and during the twenties many ranchers lost not only their cattle but their lands as well.

This possibility faced Jim McNeill. In preceding years he had added to his acreage, buying the 230-acre strip homesteaded by the Zumwalts and the adjoining Swenson section that had been leased to an early victim, Elmer Russell. He also bought a half-section that extended along the canyon in which Dockum Draw has its origin, bringing his holdings to about seven sections.

No evidence survives of any definite assurance that he would receive land adjoining his own in any division of his father's estate, but both father and son seem to have accepted this probability. Acting on this idea, he asked the Captain to deed him one and a half sections out of the northeast corner of the East Pasture. Aside from its collateral value, this tract of plains land fit our father's desire for more cultivatable acreage. The Captain concurred, but without enthusiasm, for he still held the same doubts about farming he had expressed to Henry Tilford in 1887. Some contention developed when a survey discovered a narrow vacancy strip around the northeast section, but the transfer was finally made, and in later years our father bought his part of the strip from Sidney Webb.

A reader of correspondence between the Captain and his son might conclude that there was active friction between them. Actually, a deep bond of affection united them, although differences in personalities, circumstances, and motivation created divisions in their relationship. Moreover, their letters were not written for publication, and they expressed themselves with the frankness characteristic of family communications.

Jim McNeill was never an adept writer and usually limited his communications to the business at hand. The Captain, however, included in his letters news of visitors, local happenings, and accounts of his current hunting experiences. Critical remarks concerning the ranch and its operations were a minor and infrequent portion of his communications.

Fannie McNeill had a flair for letter writing, and it is unfortunate that a more comprehensive collection of her letters to the Captain has not survived. Theirs was a fond relationship, and their correspondence was characterized by a friendly interchange of news and comment. She too was kept informed of his hunts and hunting, a practice about which she took occasion to tease him, intimating that the cost of keeping his hounds might be classified as an unproductive expense. In 1908 he countered with a statement of the year's disbursements for hunting:

Debit:		Credit:	
Eleven hounds &		Cats (Ocelots) @ $1 each	$22.00
1 fox terrier	$63.00	Coons @ 50¢ each	29.00
12 months feed, 1½ bu.		Pleasure & value	
corn meal a wk.	26.00	to dogs	250.00
Feed for 1 horse	20.00		
Total	$109.00	Total	$301.00

On November 7, 1921, he wrote his daughter-in-law: "Yes, I had another birthday, and a joyous one, too. . . . I had all the family except Jim, Fannie and the boys. . . . How I did wish for you. . . . I would like to be up there and help Jim vaccinate the cattle . . . and see the wonderful growth of the country, but I have fish to fry at home and can't leave off my duties."

This is the only surviving instance when he expressed a desire to return. But some personal impediment, never disclosed, caused him to shut himself off from the ranch.

The Zumwalt School was reactivated in the fall of 1919. Miss Imogene Barrett of Stephenville, Texas, applied for the teaching job and was gladly accepted. She had previously taught at Matador, and her motive in returning to the area was soon apparent when Cliff Bird, son of a prominent Motley County cowman, began making regular Sunday appearances at our house. She found a total enrollment of four. In addition to Randolph and myself were the Brawley boys, Edgar and Archie, whose father had bought a nearby farm originally settled by a family named English.

Meanwhile, Reese was attending the University of Illinois. He elected agriculture as his major, another manifestation of our father's long-range plans that had been transmitted to his eldest son.

Education at the Zumwalt School continued to be a hit-or-miss affair. Matrimony claimed Miss Barrett and no teacher was available for the 1921–22 term. Our father was in no position to send his younger sons to a boarding school. Fortunately, I was invited to attend school in Spur, a guest in the home of Mr. and Mrs. George S. Link, with whose son, George Jr., I had maintained a close friendship. It was for me a splendid year. The Links had a lovely home in Spur, and I was treated like a member of the family. Thereafter, Mrs. Link occupied a place in my life second only to my mother. Randolph did not fare so well, and the school year

Student body, Zumwalt School, 1919. *Clockwise from top:* Cap McNeill, Randolph McNeill, Edgar Brawley, and Archie Brawley

was added to his previous accumulation of educational blanks.

In the spring of 1922 Mr. and Mrs. Link decided to enroll George, Jr., in Kemper Military School, and Mrs. Link offered to finance my attendance there with him, evidence of her regard and generosity. I accepted gratefully. It proved a valuable experience for George and me, and a big improvement in our preparation for college.

For the McNeills, it was a time of rapid changes, weatherwise and otherwise, but optimism discounted the past and faced the future with confidence.

15. Life in the Twenties

In spite of our father's financial straits, of which he made little complaint, the early 1920s were, as observed by a teenaged boy, pleasant years at the ranch. For one thing, our mother had acquired a cook and housekeeper whose personality and capabilities deserve mention.

Jessie Hill was born in Germany, came to America with her parents as a baby, married when she was fourteen, was widowed five years later, and spent the rest of her life in domestic service. Based on a previous association, the Standifers brought her to Spur to take over the doctor's household in her own inimitable way. When the Standifers moved to a new hospital in Vernon, Hardeman County, she transferred her allegiance to the McNeills and took over housekeeping responsibilities at the ranch. Jessie could neither read nor write, but in the life-style she had developed this was a handicap of little consequence. She found her fulfillment in work and the comfort of any family to which she attached herself.

Jessie was an excellent cook and took great pride in her culinary triumphs. Her methods were unorthodox: recollection and ingenuity regulated her recipes, executed with a minimum of measuring or weighing of ingredients, practices she held in contempt.

Her system was elemental and laborious, her two hands her principal appliances. She made her own laundry soap from bacon drippings and lye, and her laundry equipment consisted of galvanized tubs, an iron wash pot in the backyard, a scrub board, and a set

Jessie Hill, 1921

of flatirons. She brought her own milk cow that she had bought out of her savings while working for the Standifers and sometimes milked it herself.

The scope of her activities was amazing. Physically, she was as strong as a man, stronger than many, and I have no recollection of any ailment she suffered more serious than a common cold, usually disregarded. In the spring she set hens in the poultry house and raised chickens by the hundreds, scorning the use of our kerosene-heated incubator and brooder. In preparation for Christmas she baked fruit cakes for all the friends she had accumulated, for which our mother cheerfully bought the ingredients. Jessie had a reputation to maintain, and she gloried in the accolades elicited by her baking.

I have no idea what our mother paid her, but it could not have been much. Her main expenditures went to furnishing her upstairs room; her attire was limited to shapeless shifts, sun bonnets, and the Russell moccasins our mother obtained for her by mail order. The Victrola she bought is still at the ranch, cherished as an antique, and the Standifer sisters she had mothered supplied her with records. Although she could not read the labels, she identified different tunes by distinctions that literate persons would not detect.

She seldom appeared to be in a hurry, maintaining a steady pace in her activities, which, for her, qualified as a vocation, and not a job. She sang at her work, usually hymns, although the religious implications of her singing were often abrogated by the language she used toward any interfering item, animal, or event. She possessed a fund of censorious phrases remarkable for accuracy and originality. No real display of wrath accompanied her invective, though delivered in the same resonant tones that characterized her singing.

The Standifers still held first claim on her, and when in 1924 they moved to another hospital they founded in Turkey, Hall County, they asked her to take over the kitchen and food services there. Mother bought her furniture, including the Victrola, since the hospital could not accommodate these items. Our father bought the milk cow, so Jessie's move included little other than her two cats, Jim and Tiger.

Concurrent with this household situation, our father had, in Lon Holleymon, similar support and services to alleviate some of the responsibilities involved in looking after the Captain's Crosby County affairs.

Reese pursued his military training in summertime R.O.T.C. camps, which usually lasted a month. When released, he often brought a friend or two for long visits with us. In 1920, it was Bob Tolman, a native of Yonkers, New York, and a veteran of World War I. In 1921, Reese and Ralph Slater, another college friend, took over a 1910 Model T Ford donated by Slater's aunt and drove it to Texas.

"Slats" was a native of Illinois. He had served in the U.S. Navy during the war, and his basic training on a sailing vessel made him a top hand around a windmill as he disdained using ladders. At the end of summer he left us in the ancient car, driving it all the way to Washington state. There he found jobs in logging camps, soon achieving distinctive status as a timber topper, the rigger who climbed, trimmed, and cut off the tops of big trees.

We had no University of Illinois guests in 1922 because Reese qualified as a member of the R.O.T.C. rifle team there and participated in the national rifle matches at Camp Perry, Michigan. He placed thirteenth in the final individual contest and had the Expert Rifleman medal pinned on by General "Black Jack" Pershing.

In 1923 Reese graduated from the University of Illinois with honors. He had carried the equivalent of a major in English along with his major in agriculture, while serving as the commanding student officer over the largest R.O.T.C. unit in the nation. Our mother came to Boonville to see me get my high school diploma from Kemper, then went on to Champaign for Reese's graduation.

Afterwards, Reese and two of his friends, Bruce McClelland and Curtis Mumford, bought a used Model T Ford and drove it to Texas with our mother as a passenger. Her mettle demonstrated the hardiness developed when much of her travel was by horse-drawn carriages along cattle trails.

These city-bred young men were no strangers to country living, for they had grown up in an era when many urban youngsters in the Midwest worked on farms in the summertime. They handled routine chores in stride. The really appealing part of their experience was the work we did on horseback. Although Curtis Mumford had spent his college vacations as a horse wrangler in Yellowstone Park, the hours spent in the saddle were no less enjoyable to him than to the others.

Curtis and I joined with Reese in a wheat farming project, for which our father had, by contract, arranged the initial plowing of 260 acres of plains grassland. As part of his education, Reese had taken a course in farm tractor maintenance and repair, and, as our first step, we set out to overhaul the Illinois tractor. Through negligence and improper use, it had been out of commission for a year. But, under Reese's guidance, the three of us rebuilt the machine; no qualified mechanics were available to work on tractors in those days.

It was quite a job, performed right on the fence row where the tractor had broken down. We had a minimum of tools and little

Branding a maverick, 1923. *From left:* Jess Freeman, Jim McNeill, and Curtis Mumford.

of the shop equipment considered essential today. But we put the tractor in a condition comparable to its delivery from the factory, and with it we started getting the plowed rough land in condition for planting.

We repaired an old grain drill (planter) built to be drawn by teams, altered the hitch to accommodate a little Ford tractor our father had bought, and with this rig planted the first wheat crop Reese and I (with Curtis's help) ever raised.

Curtis and I assisted with cattle work as needed and then virtually fulltime once wheat planting was completed. Curtis proved to be an adequate teamster and took care of that job since Steve Keith was no longer with us.

Having received a commission in the army reserve, Reese attended an encampment at Fort Sill, Oklahoma. He came back to the ranch riding on the chassis of a Model T Ford he found near the army post. He drove the 150 miles seated on the gas tank. We built a platform on the car frame, with a two-by-six board across the front for a seat. We used it to haul tractor fuel from Floydada because no wholesale oil dealers made deliveries to farms at that time. When winter came, Reese and I used it to run our trap lines, for that's how we provided ourselves with spending money. Our mother said she could tell how many skunks we had caught as soon as we topped the hill back of the ranch house.

We saved until we could buy a radio, an early model with an array of dials and adjustments on the front panel. It was powered by storage batteries, and reception came through a long aerial strung between two tall poles. With luck, we could listen to a station in Kansas City or to an announcer identified as the "Hired Hand" on Fort Worth's WBAP.

All in all, we young fellows spent an enjoyable winter in 1923–24. We enjoyed no social life with girls though, because we had neither the money nor suitable transportation for entertaining them.

In the fall of 1923 we were visited by what was, so far as I remember, the last trail herd to pass through our area. The herd boss showed up at the ranch house saying he was lost and inquiring directions. He said they had come from "down on the TP" (Texas & Pacific Railroad), about a hundred twenty-five miles to the south, and had about the same distance to travel. He had halted the herd in the northeast corner of the Half Circle S pasture next to us and wanted directions for getting through this part of the country. Our father told him to stay below the Cap Rock on a northeast course, thereby staying on ranches and avoiding the farms that had taken over the plains.

After the man left, we killed a fat mutton out of a little bunch of sheep we boys had raised from orphan lambs given us by Dr. Standifer and drove up to take a quarter to the strangers. From the looks of those cowboys, they might have come all the way from the Mexican border. They were bearded and showed the effects of

Herd approaching White River, 1923. *Riders, from left:* Bruce McClelland, Bill Putnam, and Jim McNeill

Herd leaving White River, 1923. Cap McNeill is horseman on left.

the continual wet weather prevailing that fall. Their horses were thin, with cinch sores showing and saddle sores suspected under the saddle blankets. However, the cattle were in good shape.

One other "herd" had showed up in the summer of 1922, a little bunch of forty or fifty cows attended by a seedy-looking cowboy and a lad about twelve years old. Their "chuck wagon" was a topless hack drawn by a pair of mules and driven by what was apparently the owner of the cattle and the father of the boy. He said they had come from Scurry County and were headed for his place in Motley County, which he expected to reach that day. The cowhand and the boy closely observed his inquiries about their actual location and when our father told him they were still twenty miles short of their destination, he turned to his helpers and informed

129

them, "Boys, you ain't going to get no woman's cooking tonight!"

The cowboy pulled his horse around and rode away cursing. Their rations had evidently fallen short of the quality he associated with chuck wagon cuisine.

Our 1924 wheat crop was a big success, with yields of over thirty bushels an acre, and for our labor, Reese, Curtis, and I received half the proceeds. Curtis, whose father was dean of the College of Agriculture at the University of Illinois, took his share and departed for Cornell University, where he entered graduate school in preparation for a teaching career in agricultural economics. He made the trip east as far as Kansas City by freight train, caretaker for a shipment of SR cows consigned to that market.

We had made the wheat crop under an arrangement whereby our father paid the expenses and we provided the labor. However, his financial position had deteriorated such that he was unable to continue that setup, so Reese and I took over the operation on a rental basis. With our part of the sales as a starter, a Spur bank agreed to provide us with the funds we would need. Reese signed the notes, since I was still a minor.

In January, 1924, Jim McNeill wrote to the Captain relative to his situation:

> We have never agreed on what I was to receive for looking after your interests here, for I have . . . worked under the assumed payment of $25 per month and board . . . before . . . I moved . . . to my own holdings and thought it too much for you to board us. . . .
>
> Now I have used my own horses. . . . For the past few years I have with the assistance of my boys (and one hired man paid by you) done all your work. . . .
>
> For the past three years I have furnished most of the bulls on the ranch and now you have only six bulls and I will have to sell three of these. . . .
>
> I think I have given you the best of the deal, but that is for you to say.

The wheat crop was insufficient to alleviate his problems, and in August, 1924, he appealed to the Captain: "I am going to call on you again by asking you for the one and a half sections south of the land you gave me. I am overstocked on these registered cattle, and there is no demand for them. . . . Have branded 394 [SR] calves with a few to brand that were missed. They are the best yet in age, flesh and breeding. Your cattle are getting good, wish you could see them."

The Captain responded promptly: "I am willing to let you have that one and a half sections, and at the same time let Alice and Tom Ballowe have that upper string including four and a half sections, making my pasture three miles north and south and seven miles east and west."

A tall cowboy whose name I do not recall helped me build the mile and a half of fence necessary to enclose the Captain's gift, which was mostly rough grazing land.

In the summer of 1924 the SR ranch house became an artists' colony, so to speak, with the arrival of Aunt Ola Davidson, one of the Captain's daughters, who set up a painting project there. Ola, a recognized Houston artist, brought with her two other painters, Ruth Uhler and Mary Bute, and her two children, teenaged Barbara and small son Randolph. J. P. Ballowe, son of Alice and Tom, loaded them, their equipment, and a supply of groceries in a wagon and hauled them to the deserted house.

They stayed several weeks, spending part of that time with us at our end of the ranches. Their visit became especially significant to me because Aunt Ola, ever generous, suggested that I resume my education at Rice University, inviting me to live in her Houston home while enrolled as a student. I applied for admission and was accepted for enrollment in the fall of 1925.

Reese and I had, during the winter of 1923–24, broken out more of the grassland. In the fall of 1924 we planted four hundred acres of wheat and continued breaking out sod. But the favorable weather with which we were blessed in 1923–24 did not return, and in the spring of 1925 we plowed up all the wheat except a sixty-acre strip saved for seed.

Showers in the early part of May were too late for the wheat, but encouraged us enough that we planted nearly five hundred acres of cotton and about thirty acres of Red Top sorghum. We devised a three-row planter drawn by the Illinois tractor, and I cultivated the crop with another innovation, three one-row go-devils (slide culti-vators) bolted to a heavy wooden beam.

The early summer was dry and hot, and although we got the cotton up to an acceptable stand, scanty rainfall retarded its growth; later, the rains came, and the cotton responded splendidly. But our hopes for a harvest vanished when, during the first week in October, freezing rains fell on three successive nights. Cotton bolls formed late in the growing season rotted on the stalks.

In our second year of farming — our first as entrepreneurs — Reese and I had two failures in one year. It took us the next three years to pay our debts. Our only income was from the thirty acres of Red Top sorghum that Reese managed to harvest and sell for seed.

On March 8, 1926, Uncle Charlie McNeill died in a Galveston hospital. He and Aunt Ella had spent many summer months with us, a lovable old couple that we all enjoyed. Because of some disabilities, he was not active like his brother the Captain and spent much of his time seated on our front porch.

I recall one occasion when I was about fourteen years old: I was helping my father and Floyd Wilhoit work a little bunch of cattle right in front of our house. I was riding a bay pony named Fox, let my cinch get too slack, and got bucked off when the saddle turned. The old man got a tremendous kick out of my discomfiture, and thereafter any time I encountered him he would ask: "Has the grass grown back on that place where old Fox threw you?"

When Doc Husky bought my father's mares, the black outlaw was the only gelding included. The rest had accumulated through the years, for Floyd Wilhoit was no longer available and no other capable bronc handlers had showed up to take his place. In 1924 Oscar Ford, a cowboy working on the Half Circle S Ranch, asked for the job, with the support and recommendation of Lon Holley-mon. It was a formidable task the young cowpuncher attempted, for of the eight broncs, four were eight years old and the youngest five. Sired by Boll Weevil, they quickly demonstrated a full inheritance of the bucking ability the stallion had shown years before. Oscar soon rejected one called Blanco in honor of the canyon, saying, "Mr. Mack, I managed to stay with him once, but I know I can't ever do it again!"

132

Oscar Ford on Long John, 1922

He kept the other three older horses staked to logs for forty-two days, riding them regularly, but was never able to exert enough control to make them usable. Because he was left-handed, he soon developed a huge blister in that palm, wearing thereafter a heavy glove so he could continue the "leather pulling" by which he managed to cope with the wild performances he regularly encountered.

Oscar and his buddy, a bronc rider named Rex Vermilion, finally proposed to buy the four eight year olds on credit as the nucleus of a bucking string in a planned bronc show. Their venture was unsuccessful, and Jim McNeill got his horses back in lieu of payment. One called Kiowa he gave to Bill Sauls, foreman on the Half Circle S; one called Light Foot, was broken to harness and used as a work horse; one called Long John, was still bucking in a bronc show at

133

Oscar Ford saddling a bronc, 1922

the age of twenty-one. The champion, Blanco, roamed the East Pasture for years, a spectacular piece of horseflesh as wild as any outlaw that ever lived. He was finally shot by a trapper for coyote bait.

Three of the younger horses were sold, and, of the eight, one was kept for a saddle horse. A bald-faced bay, whose dam was the gentle Nell of my childhood, was not as kindly as his mother. He was assigned to me and never threw me, for I emulated Oscar's method with a firm grip on the saddle horn.

My association with Curtis Mumford developed into a close companionship, and before he left he gave me a pair of silver mounted J. O. Bass spurs. Recollection of that gift calls to mind an episode involving the spurs.

We had loaded out a shipment of cattle at Crosbyton, and my father and I headed for Murry & Seiber's wagon yard to get our horses. As we arrived at the gate, a cowpuncher rode out on a good bay pony, leading a second horse on which his bedroll was packed. My father stopped him and asked, "How much will you take for that horse you're riding?"

"A hundred dollars," answered the cowboy, as if the price would terminate the conversation and allow him to go on his way.

"Pull your saddle off," said my father, "I'll take him."

The puncher stepped down and started loosening the cinches, while my father gave his attention to the packhorse.

"How much for this one?" he asked.

"Eighty-five dollars," was the answer.

"Take the pack off, I'll take him too," said my father, pulling out his checkbook.

As he unsaddled, the cowboy looked me over, giving particular attention to my shiny Bass Spurs. Said he, "Son, how'll you swap spurs?"

What he did not know, and Curtis did not intend, was that Mr. Bass had devised a new type of button on his spurs, and it was not a success, as I had disovered.

Cowboy fashion, I too had been making a survey of the fellow's equipment, recognizing his spurs as an older, and successful, Bass model, and replied quickly, "Even."

No ensuing conversation took place until we made the exchange and he finally commented, "Man sure can trade fast around here!"

If there was any further conversation, I do not recall it.

This incident provides opportunity to continue digressing with a brief description of an important element in cowboy equipment customary at that time — his bedroll.

The fundamental item in an adequate bedroll was the tarp (tarpaulin) in which it was wrapped. Blankets and "suggans" (quilts) were spread on one half of the tarp, leaving plenty of space between the bedding and its edges. The cowboy then pulled the other half of the tarp over his pallet and lapped the excess canvas toward the center. When this was rolled up and bound with a rope, he had a waterproof, cylindrical bundle about four feet long and two feet in diameter. Variations in diameter were determined by the amount of bedding and other articles wrapped up in the tarp, the other articles usually including a broad range of possessions.

The bedroll was the cowboy's wardrobe trunk, briefcase, armory (usually a six-shooter rusty from disuse), library, safety deposit box, laundry bag, shaving kit, and tobacco reserve. To carry this on a led horse, no pack saddle was deemed necessary. The cowboy simply draped the open roll over the horse's back, flaps under, and included the horse in the bindings.

In those earlier times, wagon yards comprised the wayside inns for people traveling horseback or in wagons, with accommodations for the horses and mules and an unfurnished bunkhouse where the traveler could spread his blankets or bedroll. I never spent a night in a wagon yard, nor do I recall SR hands being required to do so when we took herds to Crosbyton. When the cattle had been penned and sorted we unsaddled at the wagon yard and repaired to John K. Fullingim's hotel for supper and beds.

A huge man and a former Crosby County sheriff, John K. administered his own standards of conduct among the cowboys who stayed with him, one a recommendation that they shed their chaps and spurs before checking in. When a puncher named Joe Mullinax failed to observe this, the innkeeper commented, "Seems like things ain't wild enough here for some folks. Guess we will have to throw some brush in the drinking water so Joe will feel at home."

Thereafter, Joe was careful to remove his spurs before entering the place.

On December 12, 1924, our father reported SR cattle sales which indicate that the cattle market had not made any significant recovery. The total was less than $10,000, peanuts compared to present operations—and no bonanza then either. In 1925 bull sales picked up, most of them taken by Motley County buyers, including A. B. Echols, W. M. Moore, Mrs. T. E. Martin, Henry Campbell, J. C. Burleson, and L. H. Lewis. Prices were radically reduced, about half the averages in past years.

Along with our farming activities, I always took part in cattle work as needed, enjoying it much more than driving a tractor. Reese and I assisted in repairs to fences and windmills and the many other chores typical of life on a small ranch. When money and time was available, we put more grassland into cultivation, feeling that we were helping our father achieve the agricultural goals he had envisioned in 1919.

But I must confess that the prospect of college was as much an appreciation of escape from hard labor as of educational opportunity.

16. Prelude to Depression

For me, that freshman year of college was truly enjoyable for reasons beyond the relaxation involved. My acceptance into the Davidson household was unequivocal. My aunt was an outgoing, companionable woman, as was her husband, Uncle Jim, and there were no benefactor-recipient roles to be played in our relationship. I was accepted as one of the family and treated as such.

I was not the only one of the Captain's grandchildren eligible for college, and he came forward with an offer for any who would participate: $500 a year, payable $250 in September and $250 after Christmas. With free board and lodging at the Davidsons, I had it made, for at that time Rice University charged no tuition, and in 1925, $500 supplied all my other necessities.

I spent the holidays at the Captain's Liberty Hall. My saddle had been sent there in anticipation of my visit, and I accompanied him in following his hounds through the woods and in assisting my uncle and Harold Graves in working their cattle.

When the school year at Rice was completed, I took the train for Lubbock, where I spent the night with Randolph. He was enrolled at Texas Technological College, a member of the first group of registrants at that newly opened school. My journey was completed when I rode the one-a-day mixed train to Crosbyton.

My homeward return ended there. Urgency was the keynote of the occasion, for Reese had contracted to harvest a wheat crop for Sidney Webb, owner of the Bar X Ranch. The crop was ready for harvest, and when the sun rose the next morning we cranked up. By quitting time we had harvested a hundred acres of wheat.

Thereafter, eighteen hours constituted an average working day. This continued until a shower halted our operations. We took refuge from the rain in a partly loaded grain car, and I finally made contact with the trunk I had brought from Houston. It provided the first change of clothes I had enjoyed since my arrival.

Wheat harvest over, I became involved in the June branding and its aftermath: screwworms. Unlike ordinary maggots, screwworms cannot subsist on decaying flesh, but thrive on fresh blood, and each worm is equipped with a sharp hook with which to irritate the wound and promote bleeding. As a result, a mass of these loathsome blood-suckers will continually enlarge a wound, supplemented, if left alone, as more flies deposit eggs at the site. The host animal harboring such an infestation will suffer, at best, retarded growth or maiming; at worst, a slow, agonizing death.

Combatting these pests called for constant surveillance, and ranches kept riders moving among the cattle daily. In my youth we treated infested wounds with chloroform to kill the worms and then applied creosote to ward off flies. The wormy lesions stank with a putrescence that extended yards away from the victim. The whole remedial process was repulsive. Proper treatment was not performed in a few minutes; the worms did not succumb quickly, and repeated applications of "dope" were required to reach the depths of infested areas and achieve a complete kill. Encumbered with a day's supply of these elements, the cowboy's saddle, rope, pigging string (short rope for tying the animal's feet), and person soon absorbed the unpleasant aroma of his chemical burden.

In later years, a formula was devised that supplanted the chloroform and creosote. It was more effective, but carbon black was included as a base, and thereafter every item of the cowboy's gear was soon blacked with the stuff, plus many portions of his person. Discovery of an eradication process whereby sterile male flies were distributed over infested areas by airplanes virtually eliminated the pests in Texas, and, thus far, protective measures have prevented migrations from Mexico.

So far as we local McNeills were concerned, the outstanding event in 1926 was Reese's marriage, July 27, to Florence Manley. Their initial acquaintance began at the University of Illinois when alphabetical seating brought them together in an English class. Reese pursued courtship thereafter by correspondence. As a wedding present, our father gave them a Chevrolet coupe, and the trip from her home in Evanston, Illinois, constituted a honeymoon.

138

I have no idea as to Florence's expectations of a life on a Texas farm and ranch, but developments the next few years could hardly have been included in her dreams.

As implied by the fast trading incident at the Crosbyton wagon yard, the McNeills bought horses even while producing many. I grew to suspect that my father was particularly susceptible to sale opportunities involving saddle horses or milk cows, two types of livestock that seemed to hold a particular appeal. True, we had some top horses wearing other people's brands that I remember distinctly: old Nell, equine guardian of my childhood, and my blue ribbon winner, Benny; Billy the Kid and Puddinfoot, previously mentioned; Crackerjack, bought from Frank Yates and branded FY; Chief, bred by Mitt Leatherwood, lived to the ancient age of thirty-four and ducked out from most everyone who cut cattle during roundups on him; Muggins, a blue roan branded Bridle Bit, not a star at anything, but good at everything.

When O. A. "Red Mud" Lambert became manager of the Pitchfork Ranch, he saw and was captivated by a brown yearling my father had bought intending to raise him as a gelded saddle horse. Lambert said the Pitchforks was in sore need of a stallion, that he was under general cost restraints, and offered a proposition whereby my father would have his immediate choice of all their saddle horses, plus his selection from among the first colts sired by the brown yearling. My father agreed. Lambert took the yearling to the Pitchforks, and a date was set for selection from among their "cavviyard" (saddle band).

Branding was in progress at the Pitchforks, and all their horses were assembled with the chuck wagon, which was already loaded, with a four-horse team hooked on ready to move to a new location. Lambert accompanied my father as he went through the horses, answering questions about particular animals singled out for appraisal.

Finally, my father turned to Lambert. "Mud," he said, "I don't see anything here that I want."

Lambert's disappointment was evident. "Mr. Mack," he protested, "these are all the usable horses on this whole ranch. Surely we can pick out one that will make you a top mount!"

"No, Mud," was the rejoinder. "You don't have the horse I want in this bunch. He is the sorrel you have over there hitched to the chuck wagon!"

Lambert's little ruse failed, and the sorrel, named Dan, became Jim McNeill's pleasure and pride.

The second phase of the bargain was never carried out, and it is doubtful that the brown yearling ever stood as a stallion on the Pitchforks. Before that could have occurred, Lambert was supplanted by V. V. Parr, who obtained remount stallions from the government. We never knew what became of the brown yearling, for any inquiry might have created some embarrassment and misgivings, involving people not privy to Lambert's two-phased proposition.

After our disastrous cotton-raising experience in 1925, Reese and I confined most of our operations to raising wheat. Since land preparation and harvesting were accomplished in the summer months, I continued my college education and still participated in the larger part of our activities.

In 1927 Reese left as soon as harvest was over, joining Florence in Galveston, where she was awaiting the arrival of their first child. He took a job there selling cars for Sam McNeill, General Motors dealer, the son of Uncle Charlie and Aunt Ella. At an earlier age, Sam had spent a considerable amount of time at the ranch.

I took over the farming operation, plowing under the wheat stubble and preparing the land for planting, assisted by Steve Keith, teamster turned tractor driver. For me, it was a busy summer, with a minimum of time spent horseback.

In July we got the good news from Galveston. Frank Wood Manley McNeill was born on the 31st, the first grandchild for Jim and Fannie McNeill. The family returned to the ranch in time for me to resume my academic pursuits at Rice, where I had been elected managing editor of the student newspaper and had taken a room in the dormitories.

Early in 1928 the SR Camp had a new occupant. Lon Holleymon had given up that job as a dead-end situation, offering little prospect for promotion or personal opportunity. Scott Van Zant took his place, but stayed less than a year. Guy Merriman followed him and stayed a little longer, leaving in December, 1927.

Dewey Johnson moved in February 1, 1928, with his wife and

small son. Dewey grew up on the Spur Ranch, which became the SMS, where his father had been in charge of farming operations. He had years of experience on ranches, beginning when he was a youth. The tale survives that while employed by the Spurs, he was fired by the resident manager for some infraction. A herd had just left the ranch for a two-week drive to a point not identified in the story, so Dewey went to the bunkhouse, picked up his bedroll, and, following the trail herd, reported to the trail boss that he had been assigned to that crew.

The maneuver extended his employment for two weeks, since there was no communication between headquarters and the trail herd, but for a time thereafter Dewey's name was on the Spur's blacklist. For us, he proved to be a dependable and capable ranch hand, and found the situation to his liking to the extent that he stayed for twelve years.

After the wheat harvest in 1928, I notified Reese that I wanted to withdraw from our farming venture. I had been offered a job in the advertising agency operated by the Rein Company, printers and publishers. But in 1929 I graduated squarely into the Great Depression, a situation for which my classmates and I were completely unprepared. Located in a booming city and enraptured by a national economic euphoria exemplified by columnist Arthur Brisbane's catchphrase "Don't Sell America Short!", we had anticipated lives of golden opportunities and easy affluence, and found it almost impossible to realize the gravity of the situation.

When I withdrew from our farming partnership, Reese appraised the value of the equipment we had accumulated, and I agreed to wait for payment until after the 1929 harvest. Reese had planted eleven hundred acres of wheat, and his prospects were excellent. With everything in readiness for starting the harvest on Monday, a hailstorm Sunday night beat the whole crop into the ground.

The job I had been promised by the Rein Company had already been postponed indefinitely; my belated acceptance of a job offered before graduation by the Bell telephone system was rescinded, and a tentative offer by an insurance company was also withdrawn. For me, the Depression suddenly took on the form of an economic avalanche. I was broke, with no prospects of any improvement in my situation.

In preparation for the harvest, Reese had bought a Chevrolet truck, and he approached me with a proposal: take the truck and work through the wheat harvest, hauling grain from combines to elevators for half the net income. He financed the venture with a ten dollar bill and a word of advice: "If you can't get a job on this, come home before you run out of gasoline."

Before the day was out I found a job near Hereford in Deaf Smith County. The owner of the farm lived on another place, and took me on provided I would stay with the equipment at night to guard against thieves and vandals. I had collected a couple of old blankets and a scrap of canvas at the ranch for a hot roll, which was my bed for the next thirty nights. During that time I slept under a roof one showery night, my refuge a tumbledown shed.

When I returned to the ranch, Reese came up with another deal that offered employment for me and the truck. Up to this point lumberyards in the vicinity shipped in cedar fence posts by rail; Reese negotiated an arrangement with a firm operating several yards to supply them by truck. At first, we obtained posts from dealers in Palo Pinto County's cedar brakes, but soon learned to bypass them and buy directly from ranches in the hills. After making a deal with a rancher we would tear the stacks down, restack the posts according to sizes and quality, load the truck, and drive back to the point of delivery. Thereafter, Reese would proceed with his farming operations and I would haul posts until the supply purchased was used up.

It was not a profit-sharing arrangement. For my labor I was paid $4 a day plus expenses, which were limited to meals en route. Under prevailing economic conditions, it was a good job, and I could boast that I worked only twenty hours a day (the time required for a round-trip), with four hours off during which I could do anything I liked —even sleep.

On October 31, 1929, my father wrote to the Captain:

Grass has made very little growth, cows with calves rather thin. Have offered 80 head or more of cows at $45. Man offered $40, will be here when I . . . deliver the calves.

Cap, my son, wants to buy some cattle to put on wheat. We have wheat pasture as good as I ever saw, [and] we have room for more cattle.

142

> Would you sell him cows . . . and loan him the money provided he
> will pay as much as I can get [from other buyers]?

The best offer made was $30, and on November 17 I signed a note
payable to J. C. McNeill Sr. for $990, becoming owner thereby of
thirty-three cows. For the time being, I was in the cattle business.

At eighty-five, the Captain's age was beginning to show in his letters, his handwriting, and in some of his decisions. On January 23,
1930, he wrote his son Jim: "I want you . . . to pay the [property]
taxes. . . . It will not be necessary to pay the Independent [School
District] taxes. I want them to sue me. I thought about it last night.
. . . I have quit the bank as president [resigned]."

Reference is to the First State Bank of Brazoria. He had participated in its organization in 1909 and served continuously as its president for the next twenty-one years. He had become extremely deaf,
and his speech was affected, slurred, and sometimes incoherent. He
was regularly involved with the Internal Revenue Service, who had
problems with the paucity of information included in his returns,
for which he was inclined to blame his son Jim.

However, an old ledger survives among his son's papers wherein
expense accounts were kept, and its duplicate has appeared in the
Captain's home. Judging by the handwriting, Jim McNeill maintained the ledger and his wife transcribed the entries into a second
ledger and sent it to the Captain at the end of the year. Suppos-
edly, he sent it back when the current information had been utilized, and it appears that this source of information was not used
fully. As an accounting project, the records are not commendable,
but they should have been sufficient for establishing income and expense levels.

17. Adversity Alters Things

The Captain's instructions for nonpayment of school taxes arrived
too late for his son's compliance, but the matter elicited no criti-

cism. Apparently more momentous matters occupied the old man's thoughts. On June 30, 1930, the subject of these meditations may have been identified when he wrote, "I want [you] to count the cattle you have in the SR brand. I have divided my cattle and land among my children. I want [you] to count those over one year old [and] the calves not branded and I understand [from Fannie] you have already branded 300. . . . have given six sections [of land] to you, along the line I have [previously] given you."

The rest of the letter lacks clarity, but emphasizes his desire to divide the land among his surviving five children on a basis not immediately specified and to divide the livestock among them as evenly as possible. When revealed later, his plan of division proved to be well thought out, indicating that he may have established the pattern well in advance of this announcement.

In the partition, our father received the three sections lying along the west side of that already deeded him. Alice Ballowe received an additional two sections, a strip four miles long east and west and a half mile wide adjoining the south side of the four and one-half sections previously deeded her in 1924. Ola Davidson received six sections south of the Ballowe tract, a plot measuring four miles east and west and one and a half miles wide. M. E. Mitchell received a six-section strip extending six miles east and west across the south side of the ranch.

This left a four-section block in the center of these tracts, given to Jud McNeill; he was also awarded the home place on the San Bernard River. The vacant SR ranch house was located in the area given him, which also included the horse pasture George Williamson fenced in 1894.

There is no record or recollection of any dissension or criticism among the five recipients involved.

At this point the division of the Captain's land was confined to the paper on which it was outlined, for complete separation of the cattle could be effected only after surveys had established the dividing lines and fences erected thereon. It was some months before this was accomplished and, as a consequence, those portions alloted to nonresidents were operated as an informal cooperative. Alice Ballowe took her part of the cattle and the four horses assigned her, pasturing them on the four and a half sections already fenced, and putting her son, J. P. Ballowe, in charge.

Jim and Jud McNeill were handed the responsibility of representing their sisters, M. E. Mitchell and Ola Davidson. As the resident, Jim McNeill supervised operations for the other three. Dewey Johnson was retained, still living at the SR Camp, which was located on land deeded M. E. Mitchell. Jud McNeill communicated with his brother by mail, interspersed with occasional visits, usually during periods of extra activity.

Most of the fencing was done by a red-bearded contractor from Spur named Franklin, frequently referred to as "Train Robber" because of his ferocious appearance — not because of his conduct. I did not help with the surveys or fencing that completed the division of the Captain's ranch. I had pursued my trucking career during the fall, hauling bundled feed from plains farms to ranches below the Cap Rock, principally the Pitchforks, and looking after my little bunch of cows grazing Reese's wheat.

Late in February I sold the cows at a profit to John L. Birdwell, a cattleman living at Ralls, my father's friend and a long-time buyer of McNeill bulls. On March 1, 1930, I became partner in a small wholesale grocery business in Spur, financed again by my grandfather. The firm was organized by my friend, George S. Link Sr., and for the first nine months of its operation, was managed by W. R. Lewis, who had held a similar position when Bryant-Link Company operated a wholesale grocery department.

During the first several months, I was bookkeeper, warehouseman, truck driver, and billing clerk, a combination of tasks that frequently extended my working hours to a schedule similar to when I was hauling posts. Under these circumstances, I had little opportunity to take part in ranch activities.

Reese's farming operations drifted to a halt following the disastrous hail of 1929, which was followed by drastic drops in grain prices. Wheat declined to 25 cents a bushel, and no commercial market existed for the huge crop of barley he harvested in 1930. Under pressure from the bank, he delivered most of the barley to the Dickerson ranch south of Tatum, New Mexico, hauling it in his own trucks at his own expense for 10 cents a bushel. He was finally forced to sell his farming equipment, but managed to retain the Chevrolet truck and a second larger carrier. With these he operated as an independent trucker, hauling most anything most anywhere. Up to this time trucking regulations were loosely enforced in Texas.

By the end of 1929 W. R. Lewis was forced to withdraw from our grocery business. As a consequence, we had to curtail our affairs as our capitalization was reduced. I was handed the responsibility of management based on my nine months' experience. We had hired a competent bookkeeper, Enochs Pendleton, and a truck driver/ warehouseman named Barrett.

These years did produce some compensation, however, for a daughter, Virginia Frances, was born to Florence and Reese on November 12, 1930. In 1931 I fell in love, and on April 7, 1932, Maude Clemmons and I were married in her mother's home in Spur. My first contact with my bride occurred when she was first born. My mother took me with her when she went to visit her good friend, Pauline Clemmons, who had given birth to her second child, a girl. I recall the visit, but as a seven-year-old boy, bewilderment and childish embarrassment were my principal reactions on the portentous occasion.

Mrs. Clemmons made extended visits to our ranch when Maude was a child, but, following that, our contacts had progessed from seldom to none. Her evident musical talent was brought to the attention of a cousin in Dallas, composer/concert pianist David Guion, who took her under tutelage as his protege, aiming at a concert career. She attended high school in Dallas, living with her grandparents, Mr. and Mrs. Edward McAlpine.

After graduation, she continued her musical studies at the Southwestern School of Fine Arts, Guion having moved to New York, where he performed on national radio programs. His plans for Maude included the Juilliard School of Music since her application for admission had been approved. But the Depression interfered. Maude's father had died in 1923, leaving his insurance business to his wife. She continued the agency, encountering the problems that were general after 1929. When Maude was offered an opportunity to take over the piano class of a retiring music teacher in Spur, she came back to assist her mother.

Our acquaintance, meaningless in the past when she was a child and I a teenager, soon took on a new significance as congeniality ripened into matrimony. We set up housekeeping with little more than a few items of furniture for which Maude was paying by giving piano lessons to the store owner's daughters.

146

Maude McNeill, 1980

The Depression affected cattle markets even as it produced declines in other commodities, for the nation was undergoing a severe period of deflation. The demand for beef was stifled, while produc-

147

tion proceeded at an accelerated pace. The population of breeding stock increased as fewer heifers and cows were absorbed by slaughter.

By 1933 the cattle business was in desperate circumstances. The Roosevelt administration had omitted cattle as a basic commodity in establishing relief programs for agriculture, even though the government estimated that a surplus of eight million head had accumulated in the United States. Drought conditions and feed costs added to the difficulties facing cattle raisers.

A group of Texas cattlemen carried their plight to Washington, where they found strong support from Tom Connally in the Senate and Marvin Jones in the House of Representatives. These two wrote the Jones-Connally act which established a relief program for the cattle industry. A "Drought Cattle Purchase Program"[1] authorized $200 million for buying cattle, and centers were established where cattle acceptable for slaughter were butchered and the meat canned for distribution to the needy. Fifty million was authorized for purchase of cattle rejected by inspecting veterinarians. These were driven off, shot, and buried.

Under appraisal, cattle in good condition and two years old or older brought $20 a head, with values declining to $13 for those of poorer quality. Yearlings brought from $16 to $8 and calves varied from $8 to $5. Condemned mature cattle brought $12 a head, yearlings and calves $4. Condemnation was based on poor condition; diseased animals were not accepted.

In July, 1934, Jim McNeill sold, under this program, 146 head of his own cattle for an average of $12.96 a head. In the same month, Jud McNeill sold 58 head for an average of $13.79, and, in October, a consignment of 43 head, mostly calves, for an average of $7.16.

In spite of these minimal payments, the program produced beneficial results. As a market it offered about the only outlet for thin cattle unacceptable in the commercial stockyards, and these regional reception centers eliminated most shipping charges. It provided food for many destitute families and improved the general quality of cattle in the affected areas as owners were careful to dispose of the inferior animals in their herds.

The Jones-Connally Act moderated the surplus of cattle, but pro-

---

[1]"Desperate Times Called for Desperate Measures," *Cattleman Magazine,* November, 1984, pp. 151–59. Based on interview with Ernest Duke, former assistant secretary-general manager, Texas & Southwestern Cattle Raisers Association, by Larry Marshall.

ceeds from those sales were insufficient to pay costs of feed needed to maintain, under drought conditions, the livestock remaining. Through the Farm Credit Administration's Emergency Crop Loan office, arrangements were made to lend money to cattle raisers for feed purchases. Sep Smith and Carter Chase, dealers in cotton and grain, ran the local office for processing Crosby County applications. That my father used this assistance as well is evidenced by a letter approving a loan based on $1.50 per month per head for cattle and $4 a head for horses. Supplemental applications were acceptable if this allowance proved insufficient.

Following Reese's inability to continue farming, our father rented the cultivated land in 1933 to Lehigh Finch, John Dawson, and two brothers named Tree. But drought cut that arrangement short, for rainfall was insufficient to even sprout the seed put down. A new government program paying farmers for plowing up growing cotton was of no assistance, for there was none available for destruction on McNeill land. All the tenants abandoned their acreages and left the place except John Dawson, who simply had no other place to go.

In December, 1933, we received word that the Captain was ill and that death appeared imminent. Three of us left Spur for San Bernard—my father, my cousin, Sarah McNeill, Jud's daughter, who was a teacher in the Spur schools, and myself. The old man recognized none of us, and did not survive long after our arrival. He died December 17 and was buried beside his wife in the West Columbia cemetery. He was a little over a month beyond his eighty-ninth birthday.

In 1934 George Link Jr. and I rented three hundred acres of my father's farm, bought a John Deere tractor on credit, and employed John Dawson as our farmhand. The remainder of the cultivated land was rented to Clarence Ratheal. His acquisition as a resident renter proved a fortunate connection for landlord and tenant alike. It brought to the place an excellent, hard-working farmer, and enabled him, through increased acreage, the opportunity to realize his potential. Moreover, his fidelity to his landlord, addressed as "Uncle Jimmy," made his presence and performance an asset of capital value.

149

Most of the arable plains land included in the Captain's final gift was rented to Will Link, of Aspermont, Stonewall County, and H. V. Link, his son, under an arrangement whereby they received the entire first crop for putting the land in cultivation.

The government had set up a subsidy program designed to cover production costs, but something happened to the application George Link and I submitted, and no payment came our way. A similar application for the 1935 crop was also unproductive, despite repeated efforts by the local office to get some action out of Washington. Finally George Link, Sr., submitted our problem to Senator Connally, with whom he was acquainted, and the checks for both years were delivered promptly when the senator smoked out the bureaucrat who had been blocking inquiries to cover up his loss of the documents.

On Friday, April 13, 1934, James Calvin McNeill IV was born in Lubbock, where Maude had been awaiting his arrival as a guest in the home of Arthur Duggan Sr., a friend of both Mrs. Clemmons and Jim McNeill. Anticipating the event, we had obtained lodging in Lubbock for Maude and her mother for proximity to the doctor and a hospital, but Mr. Duggan insisted on moving them to his home as soon as he learned of their presence and their mission. It was a splendid example of hospitality as practiced in those troubled times.

Although the Captain's gifts of land, beginning in 1922, averted financial disaster for Jim McNeill, the Depression found him still burdened with debt for which there was no relief. By 1937 the same succession of drought and depressed prices found him facing financial disaster again.

The adjoining Half Circle S Ranch had come into the hands of Morgan Jones, bachelor financier, and upon his death the inheritance passed to nephews and nieces, most of whom lived in England. But one, Percy Jones, who was present in the United States, was named executor of the estate and agreed to buy acreage from this neighbor sufficient to get him "out of his tight" and extend his use of the land under a lease.

A strip of plains land bought from Ed Hutson, plus the half section lying along the canyon where Dockum Draw had its origin was ceded to the Texas Land & Mortgage Company in order for the Jones estate's acquisition to be in a block. Offsetting this, the Jones estate acquired a section and a half of the Captain's gift, being the southeastern part of that tract, most of it rough grazing land.

This development proved to be, for Jim McNeill, deliverance from twenty years of financial hardships, and Percy Jones's intervention provided him with a fresh opportunity that quickly bore fruit. The original Jones/McNeill lease, dated October 1, 1937, has been regularly renewed through close to half a century. When the Morgan Jones estate was divided among the heirs, the land involved here was awarded to Percy's youngest brother Roland, and the friendly connection between the two families has continued to the present.

The severity of the financial situation affecting ranchmen in the decade following World War I and the subsequent Depression is illustrated by the fact that every ranch that adjoined us went out of business. Elmer Russell, the Putmans, Frank Corn's Half Circle S, and Sidney Webb's Bar X all failed to survive.

Failures were not confined to our immediate vicinity. Among our associates, in Kent County Ed Cairn's cattle bearing his Paddle brand were sold by his creditors, and his neighbors, Bert and Chalk Brown, lost the land and cattle they inherited from Boley Brown, their father. Over in Lubbock County, George Boles's outstanding herd of registered Herefords and his highly improved ranch were lost to satisfy creditors. This struck close to us, for the Boleses were particular friends and their ranch the model toward which Jim McNeill aspired.

These instances were not isolated even though they are limited to our neighbors and friends, for the same thing was happening to cattle raisers all over the grasslands of the West. The Captain's early gifts of debt-free land were the means by which our little ranch survived.

The change in our father's economic situation was matched the same year with the sale of the wholesale grocery business to the Hestand-Kimbell Grocery Company, headquartered in Lubbock. That company continued it at Spur as a branch house, and I was employed as manager. Reese, who had joined me, assumed most of the sales contacts in the area. In this new regime, my responsibilities were reduced to the point where I could participate again in affairs at the ranch. I took over the records of my father's registered Herefords and, having acquired from a debtor a big gray horse and a saddle, took part in working cattle as my schedule would permit.

Such an occasion developed soon after this change in my affairs. I went by our house to change clothes, bearing in mind a pair of Justin boots I bought in 1929 while working in the wheat harvest. I told Maude my plans, and she assisted my hasty change to suitable apparel. But a thorough search of our tiny house failed to produce the boots I had in mind. They were never found, then or thereafter, and I finally concluded that somehow they had been lost. It was quite a while before Maude felt it safe to tell me, mirthfully, that after years of disuse, she decided the boots were superfluous and had traded them to the yardman. The diligence she manifested in our search indicated histrionic abilities with which she had not been accorded recognition.

The first delivery of McNeill cattle to a distant market by truck occurred in June, 1936. Seven cows belonging to Jim and Jud McNeill were hauled to Fort Worth by a trucker named Bilberry, who collected $33.45, calculated on a rate of 50 cents per hundredweight. The cows sold for an average of $4.61 per hundredweight indicating some improvement over 1934 prices.

The earliest sale of McNeill cattle through a local auction barn occurred in October, 1940, according to surviving records. Seventeen cut-back steer and heifer calves were sold by the Lubbock Auction & Commission Company, operated by J. M. "Bunk" Mullins, Henry Lawson, and Claud Keeton. The calves weighed, on average, 311 lbs. and sold for $9.25 a hundredweight, a marked improvement over 1934 prices.

Improvement in the registered herd was Jim McNeill's major interest, and he set about doing so by introducing new blood from other breeders. The purchase of a bull named The Prince Domino 5th from Jack Frost's White Hat Ranch in Fisher County proved a progressive step in upgrading the cattle, and a close and friendly association with Arthur Burnside, of Iowa Park, Wichita County, effected some beneficial exchanges.

152

18. World Conflict Again

The loose cooperative involving M. E. Mitchell, Ola Davidson, and Jud McNeill slowly disintegrated after the lands had been fenced and the cattle separated. Ola was making plans for a tour of Europe's art galleries and hoping to finance her trip out of her cattle interests. Her sister, Alice Ballowe, had already disposed of her Spanish Y cattle and leased her land to John L. Birdwell. Ola soon followed suit and departed for Europe in 1937. By that time the Ballowe and Davidson lands had been leased to Stanton Brunson.

Cattle raising in Brazoria and Crosby counties was marked by some fundamental differences, reflected in the principal markets for those areas. It is apparent that these differences created doubts in Jud McNeill, but it was contrary to his tolerant character to contest openly the cattle-raising ideas of his brother Jim. At any rate, Jud and his son disposed of the Hereford cattle inherited from the Captain. In their place they stocked their pastures with 160 head of mixed-breed cows bought from Johnny Savell of Alvin, Texas, including in the final truckload four registered Brahman bulls.

L. J. "Jordie" McNeill Jr. was graduated from A&M University in 1938 and included in the Crosby County cattle business with his father. He spent a large part of his time thereafter with Uncle Jim and Aunt Fannie, a great help in conducting the varied cattle interests included at the ranch.

Dewey Johnson's residence at the SR Camp ended about 1940. He was hired by Stanton Brunson and relocated on the Ballowe place, and for a time the camp was vacant. One evening I received a phone call at my home in Spur, and was surprised to learn the caller was Lon Holleymon. It had been fifteen years since we had any word from him. He told me his wife had been dead for some time, that his children were scattered on West Texas ranches, and that he still dreamed of the SR Camp and Blanco Canyon. When I told him the place was unoccupied, he asked if there was any chance for him to return to it. Though age had slowed him down, he would like an opportunity to make himself useful.

My father welcomed the idea, for a wartime labor shortage was upon us. Soon Lon established bachelor quarters at the place he had left, reluctantly, in hopes of providing a better situation for his family. He was assigned to looking after Jud and Jordie McNeill's

South Texas cattle ("Orange Blossoms" Lon called them) and the remnant of Hereford cows belonging to M. E. Mitchell.

The year 1941 proved to be the wettest on record in Dickens and Crosby counties with over forty inches of rainfall. We had no deluges such as George Williamson reported in 1899, but intermittent showers were general and frequent over the area.

Under the current federal farm program, operators in compliance were required to plant cover crops on lands taken out of production. Although these crops could not be grazed, they could be salvaged as fodder by baling or other means of preservation. Clarence planted the idle acres to Red Top sorghum that grew tall and rank watered by the unusual rainfall.

My father chose to store this godsend in the ground and had bulldozers dig three pits at locations along the upper edge of the Cap Rock. In aggregate, these pits had a total length of about two hundred feet and were about eight feet deep and fifteen wide. The cane was harvested with a machine that chopped the stalks and leaves into two-inch sections, which were blown into trailers hitched on behind. These were unloaded in the pits where a tractor packed them to exclude the air. Estimates as to the amount of fodder put away are now forgotten, but the total amounted to several hundred tons.

Jim McNeill was proud of the pit silo project. But, strangely enough, he never fed any appreciable amount of this huge reserve to his own cattle. Apparently he felt that it represented a "hole card" to be preserved until drought years such as 1918 and 1934 might create similar scanty range conditions.

As 1941 drew to a close, Reese and I both submitted resignations to the Hestand-Kimbell Grocery Company, though Walter Hestand persuaded me to remain for another six months. We turned our attention to the farm and started a hog-feeding project there, building a barn and granary with lumber salvaged from the SR ranch house. It had been torn down when, after fifty years (including some twenty years of almost total vacancy), it was about to collapse into the basement.

Arthur Burnside, Hereford breeder at Iowa Park, persuaded Reese to come into his life insurance business, and Reese made good use of the contacts his work in grocery sales had produced in the six-county area he had traveled. It was a blessed relief for both of us. I devoted my time to the livestock and looking after my crops.

Jud McNeill's concepts of cattle raising included the Captain's opposition to supplemental feeding in winter, and he directed that this feeding be omitted. As a consequence, they fared rather badly, and in winter Lon would carry a little cotton seed cake on his saddle for the benefit of a few especially weak cows. In tending to such a hardship victim, he carelessly exposed himself to one of the Brahman bulls and was injured when the bull attacked him.

The accident occurred at Jud McNeill's pens, but Lon managed to get on his horse and ride the five miles to our home place. Mother and Randolph helped get him off his horse and into bed. He was badly bruised, for the bull had mauled him about on the ground following the initial assault. Although no bones were broken, he was unable to return to the SR Camp for several weeks.

In February, 1942, Jordie McNeill was called into service as an officer in the Reserve Corps. Jud decided to replace Jordie himself in looking after their Crosby County property, but that ended when, on a visit to the ranch, he suffered a severe heart attack. When he returned home to the San Bernard, his doctor advised against further trips to the ranch because of the long trips and the difference in altitude. As a consequence, care of the L. J. McNeill cattle was again committed to my father.

Lon's encounter with the Brahman bull reminded his employer of the man's built-in disregard for his own safety, and he became concerned about Lon's solitary occupation of the SR Camp, where his only mode of travel or communication was horseback. Thus, although aware of Lon's attachment to the place, my father introduced the idea of my taking over that part of the ranch, since I had cattle located there, and moving Lon in with the family at the Alamo Stock Farm.

We set about some improvements at the SR Camp, looking ahead to a time when I might have my family there. We had the house ready by the time school was over at Spur and moved in with our two boys, eight-year-old Jimmy and four-year-old George David. It was Maude's first experience at ranch life as lived by camp hands, and she enjoyed the holiday aspect of our summer residence. The boys were delighted with the situation, attaching themselves to the camp and its environs that had, and have, infected others who have occupied the place. With horses to ride, a shady grove in which to play, and a spring-fed swimming hole nearby, their major desires were fulfilled.

In 1942 my aunt, M. E. Mitchell, notified her brother Jim that she wanted to sell the cows remaining to her and lease the rest of her land; she had already leased him a two-section pasture watered by the Waddell Draw. Her herd had been reduced to forty nine-year-old Hereford cows, which I bought, adding them to cattle I already had in a pasture I had leased from her.

When I was twelve years old my father gave me a registered Hereford heifer named Twilight. Although he kept up the registrations on the calves accruing, the certificates carried my name as the owner. However, I received none of the proceeds from sales, and knowing of his financial difficulties, expected none. I did question the apparent fallacy of showing me as the owner, for, since I held no stock in the American Hereford Association, the fees for registrations and transfers were higher. He never gave me an adequate answer, but was always apologetic for having branded the cattle with the C on the jaw that identified them as his. The mortgages he signed included all livestock bearing that brand, plus the increase, and he felt bound to honor that commitment to his creditors, in full. His ultimate purpose emerged when he told me to pick up all the cows registered in my name and move them to the Sand Rock pasture at the SR Camp. I was now, in a small way, in the registered cattle business. I did so gladly, taking with them on loan a good bull from the group he maintained.

He, Reese, and I had been buying feeder pigs, and recalling how hogs fatten on acorns, we decided to take advantage of the shinnery (shin oak) growing along Waddell Draw. Accordingly, one cool morning we drove 190 shoats about three miles off the Cap Rock, herding them horseback like cattle and turning them loose at the first waterhole.

To localize them, we set up a self-feeder near the creek and filled it with threshed grain. Our venture progressed nicely, and the combination of acorns, mesquite beans, and grain produced pork at a minimum cost per pound of gain. Later, we conducted a swine roundup, but gathered only about a hundred head; the rest of them had become too wild to be herded with the rest. So we marketed our more congenial porkers and laid plans for recovering the outlaws.

We built a stout pen around the feeder with a gate in one corner, from which we extended a wing—a line of fence that would force any hogs to go through the gate that had been herded in that closely. Thereafter, horseback, I would conduct a slow drive up the creek toward the pen, making a lot of noise to keep the hogs moving ahead of me in the right direction. When a considerable number had gone in the pen, I would shut the gate, and we would load our selection of marketable hogs through a chute we had built for the purpose. This procedure succeeded until we had recovered most of our strays, but some of the hogs had become too wild to be driven to the pen.

Knowing that these outlaws came to the feeder at night, I installed a smaller gate that opened toward the interior of the pen. Normally, I fastened this little gate ajar until we elected to sell some more hogs. Then, late in the afternoon, I would let it swing shut, with a screen door spring holding it closed. The hogs had no difficulty pushing the gate open to get at the feed, but the spring kept it closed after they had gone through. Early the next morning, my father would meet me at the pen and we would load his pickup with marketable hogs.

Ours were not the only hogs ranging along Waddell Draw and White River to the COE Spring, and we arrived at an understanding with our neighbors on the adjoining ranch according to which hogs were treated as wild game. Any porkers captured by the ranches involved belonged to the captor. This situation still exists, and wild hogs continue to inhabit the area. On occasion, hog hunts convert some of these unrestrained porkers to domestic usage.

Maude and the boys moved back to Spur when school started in September, and I embarked on a bachelor existence at the camp, visiting the family on weekends, weather permitting. It was a rather restricted life-style: cooking on a wood-burning stove, with no refrigeration and no electrical appliances other than a battery-powered radio.

Most of the convenience foods so plentiful today were yet to be developed, and those available were not adapted to circumstances at the camp. I baked biscuits according to a recipe I found on a

KC Baking Powder can, supplemented with corn bread for which Maude had given me a formula so flexible it survived all my careless errors. The cook stove provided a permanent location for the bean pot, and the frijoles got a little more cooking every time the fire was lighted. I kept a domesticated range cow, providing plenty of fresh milk for my table. With stewed dried fruit for dessert, my menu was princely compared with that at the dugout in the 1890s.

Saddle stock was in short supply. Jim McNeill's penchant for buying horses had receded with the years, and the mounts available had, for the most part, outlived their more useful ages. A good sorrel pony I had picked up went bad in his knees, and an old streak-faced horse Frank Corn donated was plagued with scabrous allergies that rendered him useless in warm weather months. My father had warned me to stay off a big brown three-year-old that Lon had left behind when he moved away from the camp. He said the horse had been bought in the expectation that he would be useful to Lon, but was rejected as unmanageable and slated to go back to the sale ring when convenient.

It was never my intention to qualify as a "bronc stomper," following my father's advice that "There are enough damn fools in the world to ride all the broncs." Nevertheless, I saddled that horse one hot, muggy afternoon, succeeded in suppressing his attempt to buck, and took him on a long, sweaty ride across the canyon. The experiment was successful. I did not get thrown, and in time the horse proved acceptable for working cattle and roping screwworm-infested calves.

Lon was never happy away from the SR Camp and left early in the fall of 1943. Upon his departure I took on the care of cattle belonging to Jud and Jordie, drawing wages which they split with my father since the home place was included in the range of my activities. In line with practices the Captain established, the salary assigned me was $50 a month, with no fringe benefits such as horse feed, grub, or gasoline. I assumed that the time I devoted to looking after my own livestock absorbed those items of expense and was happy to be of help in a tight situation. I had hired Gene Hardin to look after my farming operations, with Clarence Ratheal supervising the job.

Any assumption that I was unhappy with my circumstances would be incorrect, for I was back on the land I loved, doing the things

I liked to do. My hours were from "see to see," dawn to dusk, and, under wartime conditions, most of the time I worked alone.

On November 23, 1943, Maude and I welcomed our first daughter, named Ann Fentress, born in Lubbock's St. Mary's Hospital. Then on May 1, 1944, Maude, baby Ann, and son George joined me at the SR Camp. Jimmy stayed with his grandmother, Mrs. Clemmons, until the end of the school year, hitching rides with the mail carrier for weekends with us.

The end of World War II brought about a welcome moderation in the availability of consumer goods. Eventually we even introduced electricity at the camp, with a gasoline-powered generator producing current enough for Maude to use her electric iron.

Maude managed our household very competently in spite of shortages and isolation, but experienced a severe case of cabin fever in January, 1946, when temperatures plunged below the zero mark. Pent up in a small house with a baby and two active little boys, her anxieties multiplied as time passed by with no improvement in the weather. Snowdrifts blocked the road up the Cap Rock, our only access to the outside world. The water in our storage tank became solid ice, and only by thawing out the windmill for short periods during the day was I able to fill buckets and other containers by running a garden hose through the bathroom window.

When the longed-for thaw arrived, Jimmy and I managed to get to town for groceries and mail, but fighting the mud as we returned, our 1941 Oldsmobile stalled inside the pasture gate, and afoot we toted our supplies the remaining two miles to the house.

With Jordie in the army and his father restrained by the doctors, my father and I looked after their cattle according to practices we supposed acceptable to them. Jud had, in October, 1944, expressed a desire to retain half-Brahman heifers to replace their mixed-breed cows. We accomplished this when overgrazed pastures with no supplementary feed brought about reduced calf crops, and many of the cows that calved went off in condition and did not breed again. As a result, the cows that did not produce calves fattened and were sold; wartime prices enabled us to get an average of $100 a head for cows bought from Johnny Savell for just $35.

As the cattle improved in Brahman characteristics, they deteriorated in conduct, becoming wilder and more unmanageable as their

Zebu breeding became evident. Fortunately, neighborly assistance was available, and without the cooperation of the crew at Brunson's L7 Ranch I would have had serious problems working the L. J. Mc-Neill cattle. W. W. Brunson, Stanton's father, had leased the Morgan Jones land that was originally the South Two Buckle pasture, and had placed his brother Gilbert there as ranch manager.

Gilbert proved to be a cordial friend and an accommodating neighbor. His years of experience and the regard accorded him by cowhands attracted top performers to his employ. Calvin B. "Bud" Leatherwood, named for the Captain and raised on an East Plains farm, was often available. Bud's real interest was in cattle raising, although by inheritance a farmer, and my father shared my dependence on him. Our association was based on a three-generation relationship, for our fathers and grandfathers had been close friends.

When veterans of World War II came home, the crew assembled at the L7 Ranch was, in my experience, the best group of cowboys with whom I ever worked. Gilbert's two sons, Curtis and Willis, were top hands, as were Red Whatley, Dutch Hines, Orvie Jones, Willard Davis, and Billy Robertson. Billy Kirk, of the Hank Smith family, was frequently included, as was my standby, Bud Leatherwood. Red Parker, who preferred the isolation of Brunson's River Camp, and Bill Howell, Gilbert's son-in-law, proficient at many things, rounded out the list of stars.

I was careful to participate in roundups in L7 pastures that adjoined us and in more distant areas when my presence was indicated. Then, when I needed to work the L. J. McNeill cattle, Gilbert would send a complete crew to assist. I also had a reciprocating relationship with Gilbert's nephew, Stanton Brunson, who had the Davidson and Ballowe pastures under lease. Altogether, we were involved in a pleasant and cooperative arrangement along Blanco Canyon and White River, a setup that has continued through the years.

In 1946 Jordie was released from military service, and, accompanied by his wife, Mary Eloise, came to the ranch in time for branding. He told me that he and his father wanted to consolidate their cattle business closer to home and that he would like to sell their Crosby County cattle and lease the land.

He found a buyer immediately, for I wanted the lease badly, and the lump sum he named for purchase of the cattle was fair. The deal enabled me personally to take under lease eight sections of the Captain's original range. In all, it appeared to be a propitious time for cattle raisers, and my small enterprise headed in a promising direction.

19. Vicissitudes of Fortune

Postwar cattle prices, freed from artificial restraints, advanced in step with government policies designed to prevent a recession. The weather in our area cooperated, and the phenomenal rainfall of 1941 was followed by conditions generally favorable for farms and grass-lands.

By 1949 I had disposed of all the Brahman-type cattle acquired from Jordie and his father, other than a few outlaws that continually escaped our roundups. Thereafter I bought and sold yearlings, retaining some heifers to reestablish a breeding herd. I also made connection with a commission man in Fort Worth, who, on request, furnished me with thin cows that I could fatten on wheat pasture or grass.

We continued our residence at the SR Camp, which created problems in school attendance for the little boys. In 1946 we managed to rent an old house in Crosbyton, remembered for its one closet where I could check on the weather by looking through holes in the roof located above it. We moved back to the camp as soon as school was out. Shortly thereafter we bought a Crosbyton house just across the street from our friends the Covingtons and only two blocks from the school.

A winter storm in January, 1949, covered the ground with ice that did not melt for six weeks. I had cows in the pens at the SR Camp and was feeding them from the silage put in the pits in 1941. I could load about three thousand pounds of silage in my red International pickup, and, since that was the daily capacity of the cows, I had to make the trip every day. Only one time did I fail them, when a breakdown deterred me.

Cattle survived the icy conditions surprisingly well. Most of Jim McNeill's registered Herefords were at the farm when the storm struck, grazing wheat and sorghum stalks. They retreated off the Cap Rock when the gates were opened, finding shelter and grass in the hills below. My losses were confined to two Brahman heifers, a yearling that froze to death and a fat two year old, evidently injured when she slipped and fell on the ice.

My father died suddenly in May, 1949, at Reese's house in Spur, where, apparently in good health and high spirits, he had stopped for a visit with his daughter-in-law Florence. It was assumed that he suffered a massive heart attack, though evidence of heart trouble had not previously been detected. He was seventy-four years old. He was buried at Spur, becoming the first McNeill laid to rest in the family plot established in the cemetery there.

Jud McNeill did not long outlive his brother. He died in December, 1950, victim of a heart condition that had limited his activities since 1942. He was seventy years old.

Since Reese was heavily involved in his seed business that extended from Kansas to Arizona to South Texas, and since I had been closely associated with our father's cattle business, I was appointed administrator of the estate and took on that responsibility by mutual consent, for our father died intestate.

He left a commendable herd of registered Herefords that he had developed in the thirty-seven years since his initial purchase of the Armour cows. However, his performance as a merchant did not match his competence as a breeder, and he had not established a market with sufficient breadth to assure a reliable demand for his bulls. He never advertised, and the exhibitions of his cattle were limited to a few entries at the Dickens County fair when that small exposition was in operation.

He was somewhat handicapped in acquiring good herd sires by the limits of his means, but managed to obtain bulls that improved his cattle. The 1938 purchase of the bull The Prince Domino 5th was a significant step forward.

He had assisted Arthur Burnside, of Iowa Park, in selecting a Hereford herd, and they became fast friends. Burnside bought a bull from a Fort Worth breeder whose concentration of Prince Domino bloodlines focused on a bull named Prince Domino Return, and several Burnside bulls produced thereafter found their way into our father's possession. Two, in particular, proved to be excellent sires.

Jim McNeill just a few days before his death, 1949

It was a fortuitous time for me to assume the management of the cattle, for the cycle that dominates the cattle business was in ascendancy. The prices that continued advancing after wartime restrictions were removed generated a rush of people anxious to become cattle raisers.

At the time of his death, our father did not have many young bulls of serviceable ages, but a fine crop of bull calves was already on the ground. Before summer was gone buyers were already anticipating our weaning dates.

The first was John Birdwell, Jim McNeill's friend and a regular purchaser, who came, looked, and told me to notify him when we cut these early calves off from the cows. He wanted ten and asked

163

me to reserve the "first pick," a request I was happy to grant. When that time arrived, he took twelve, while a second buyer sat on the corral fence awaiting his turn.

These calves were dropped in the preceding fall and were weaned in the late summer. A steady demand for these young bulls continued in spite of my raising prices to match the progress of a seller's market. Before the fall was over, we were sold out of this early calf crop, and when we weaned those dropped in the spring, buyers were ready to take them off our hands.

Range conditions were excellent in 1950 and I notified our Fort Worth commission man to start sending thin cows as they became available, planning to stock one of the L. J. McNeill pastures with them. The only animal left there was a white Brahman cow that had escaped the drive when we moved the cattle out of that place. Sam Gannon was working for us, and together he and I undertook the job of moving her into another pasture.

Soon after we started our search I rode up on the cow in some low mesquite bushes and took after her, full speed, in an effort to turn her toward the pens. The chase did not last long, for my horse stepped in a grass-covered hole and fell, headlong. I was thrown clear of him, but in his cartwheeling velocity he caught up with me as I somersaulted along, and I received a smashing blow on my right shoulder that knocked all the wind out of my lungs.

Sam, who was about two hundred yards away, did not actually see my tumble but guessed what had happened when I suddenly disappeared in the brush and a cloud of dust bloomed where I had dropped out of sight. When he got to me I was crawling around on hands and knees, struggling to recover my breath. I finally succeeded, and we began taking stock of my condition, which, in our estimation, included a broken right shoulder.

Sam tied our bandanna handkerchiefs together, fashioning a sling to support my right arm, for I found the weight of it unbearable. He changed the saddles on our horses, for the black I was riding was a treacherous beast, while the one he was riding was quite gentle. He helped me to mount, and left in a long lope, going to get the pickup we had left some two miles away. Our plan called for me to ride to a point atop the Cap Rock reckoned as the nearest place available to our vehicle.

It was a painful ride of about a mile and a half. When I arrived

Sam took me to the hospital in Crosbyton, where a technician told me to get on the x-ray table while she called Dr. Milo Snodgrass. I did so, still wearing my chaps and spurs, but after the pictures were developed they refused my offer to climb down; instead, they eased me off on a sheet, for my injury was not a broken shoulder but a broken back.

My recovery was rapid. After a few days of immobility, Dr. Snodgrass fitted me with a body cast covering everything from my armpits to my hips. A month later I graduated to a brace, and after another month was back in the saddle, reminded at times to slow down when a little too much action caused the long steel stays to pinch my tail.

Encouraged by improvements in the cattle business, we introduced some new practices, installing self-feeders in some of the pastures constructed so only the calves had access to the feed. Also, in hopes of widening the scope of prospective customers, I investigated regional associations of Hereford breeders, taking membership in two: a comparatively small one at Sweetwater and a statewide organization headquartered in Fort Worth.

The Texas Hereford Association had come under the management of Henry Elder, who began his career as a teacher of vocational agriculture in the little East Plains high school at McAdoo. There he soon attracted attention when his student projects consistently won over larger schools in the region. In like manner, Henry's progress to the executive office in the state association signalled the awakening of that self-possessed organization to an expanded membership and an active promotional program. We joined, and, as a member, never had occasion to regret our participation as long as Henry Elder continued as its executive secretary.

Our first venture into a consignment auction sale was at Sweetwater in 1950. The three bull yearlings we nominated stood well in their class and sold at satisfactory prices. The ranch profited by acquaintances made and the cooperation that existed among the breeders contacted.

In 1951 what began as a market decline encountered resistance in the optimism characteristic of cattlemen, the inborn hope that any drought will soon terminate in beneficial rains, and that a falling market will soon revive itself. What we could not foresee was

165

that the dry weather then prevailing over the western United States marked the beginning of a drought that would continue for the next six years. The combination of overpopulation of cattle and a reduction in the grazing available nationally, created a situation that worsened annually to the point of disaster.

In spite of these circumstances, we survived the ordeal in relatively good shape. As usual, cheap feed constituted the principal item in the solution of our problems, and through some fortuitous factors we had access to a supply unavailable to many cattle raisers.

Reese had expanded his seed business to the point where he was one of the largest grain sorghum dealers in Texas. Much of the seed he marketed was produced under contracts with farmers, in addition to seeds he grew himself on leased, irrigated acreages. Spur was the headquarters for his sales efforts, and he established there a processing plant where these field-harvested seeds were recleaned, sacked, and tested for germination. In recleaning, cracked and imperfect grains were eliminated, then milled and fortified with high-protein additives to make excellent supplementary feeds for our calves and yearlings.

We also took part in a program whereby surplus grain in government warehouses was sold to cattle owners at reduced prices. We expanded our participation in breeders' associations and in the consignment of bulls and heifers to the sales they conducted. In addition to Sweetwater, we sold registered cattle at Abilene, Big Spring, Childress, and Amarillo.

The market situation was harder on breeders of registered cattle than on those whose herds were limited to commercial animals. Henry Elder responded to this predicament with his usual discernment and energy, and the Texas Hereford Association began "Round Up" sales at Fort Worth, open to all members with no requirements for quality or condition.

Breeders took full responsibility for their offerings, but were guaranteed an outlet for cattle for which they previously had none. The response was immediate and extensive, and several of these sales were conducted during the years of drought and depressed markets. Most of the cattle consigned were in no better than fair condition, and the general level of quality was substandard.

But knowing that these sales were held at a principal cattle market and that attendance would be from a broad area, I felt that among them would be cattlemen interested in well-bred, serviceable young bulls in good flesh, and made consignments based on that assumption. It proved correct, and our bulls (plus a few heifers) sold for prices that compared favorably with those obtained in the sales limited to selected entries.

The exposure we obtained in these sales put us in contact with out-of-state buyers. As a result we sold fifty heifers to a man from Connecticut for his farms in North Carolina, twenty to the University of Florida, and ten to a Fort Worth businessman who had bought six of our heifers in a Round Up sale.

These activities are representative of years of hard work, for our schedule of feeding and conditioning cattle for the sales was a strenuous one. I had recovered fully from my injury and was left with nothing more serious than a slight detour in my spinal column, observable only by x-ray.

Most of the time I had adequate help, for Bud Leatherwood had sold his farming equipment and leased his land. After Sam Gannon left, he looked after the cattle in the pastures. I had hired Graden Bass to attend to my farming, and he proved a big help when we were making consignment sales. These sales happened in the winter and early spring, a slack time for tractor drivers. Bass was especially handy at washing bulls, a rather lively chore, since we were haltering and grooming bulls weighing a thousand to twelve hundred pounds that were range raised and unaccustomed to such familiarities.

Son Jimmy graduated from Kemper Military School in 1951. He developed a peptic ulcer soon thereafter, and on the advice of Dr. Snodgrass, did not enter college that fall. Consequently, we had his assistance through most of the first year of the drought. He enrolled at Texas Technological College in the fall of 1952.

In June, 1953, we experienced a scare when we lost eight registered cows and an old Burnside bull in the small pasture where Ed Hutson's half-dugout had been located. Failure of a float valve regulating the water level in a stock tub apparently caused the disaster. The facts were rather confusing, for the survivors were not in a state indicating extreme thirst, and the carcasses were widely scattered away from the water tub.

Bill Romane, veterinarian and friend, went with me to investigate the situation. We made note of wet moss in the bottom of the stock tub and took samples from the stomach of a cow that was not long dead. Bill suggested anthrax as a possibility, advising that we bury the dead cows to reduce the possibility of spreading the contagion. We put two tractors to work and soon found just how difficult it is to bury the swollen body of a thousand-pound cow, digging in ground hardened by dry weather.

We sent samples taken from the dead cow to the Texas Extension Service's laboratory at College Station, and, in time, received a report that alleviated our fears. According to analysis, the cause of death was botulism that had developed in the moss as it rotted in the stock tub, and some of the cattle had eaten of the wet residue.

We took no more chances at that location, allowing the cattle thereafter free access to the main storage tank. Our father had enclosed it so he could enjoy fishing there while irrigating a garden he cultivated at this windmill, two miles from the ranch house.

In 1951 Carl Craddock, of Pawhuska, Oklahoma leased the North Cat pasture of the Morgan Jones ranch, which had come to be known as the L7 Ranch in deference to Brunson's long occupation of the place. The pasture offered no living accommodations other than the River Camp, a rather primitive dwelling whose basic structures consisted of two condemned boxcars. So Craddock approached me about the vacant SR Camp, and we made a deal.

In 1952 Craddock added the South Cat pasture to his leasehold, increasing it to over forty sections. He had established himself as a capable cowman and a good neighbor. In 1953 the decline in cattle prices accelerated, dropping to a level 50 percent below those prevailing in 1950–51. But just before this big drop, Craddock sold the cattle and transferred the lease to a firm in California.

The Whittaker Company, manufacturers, were newcomers to the cattle business, and their innocence enabled Craddock, in the vernacular of the West, to "dodge lightning." The newcomers lodged their hands in the SR Camp.

A three-inch rain in May, 1955, filled the playa lakes at the farm, altering drought conditions. Since Clarence Ratheal had moved to his own place, Reese and I had divided the cultivated land between us, and we both tried pumping water from the lakes in the dry weeks that followed. I tried irrigating cotton and found it a laborious task, for the rows were laid out in a contour pattern designed to maintain a constant level. Coaxing water to flow over these level courses proved to be a job requiring constant vigilance and lots of shovelling.

Reese chose to water some forage sorghum and simply flooded the terraces, a process that could not be adapted to the cotton. His production was fantastic, the sorghum growing to seven- and eight-foot heights. It was a development important to our cattle, for seed production was his objective. The tremendous amount of fodder accumulated as a byproduct helped immensely in the dry winter of 1955–56.

A particularly dry year followed 1955. Jimmy withdrew from Texas Tech and tried his hand at farming some of the land I was using. Moisture sufficient for planting did not come, and late in May he "dry planted" cotton in hopes that a timely shower would sprout the seed. The rain just never came, and this year shared with 1933 the distinction of being, on our ranch, a time when drought was so severe that crops could not even be started. Ranges deteriorated from year to year, leaving bare areas similar to those that developed in 1918. The local Soil Conservation office worked out a five-year plan for us, predicated on improved weather conditions — when and if that might occur.

The situation my father prepared for in 1941 came to pass in the winter of 1956–57, seven years after his death. Drought conditions had radically reduced the native forage in our pastures, and we supplemented it generously with the silage that had been buried for fifteen years. Its dark brown color and acrid odor found no objectors among the cattle. We fed twenty pounds a day per cow, and it seemed to produce an appetite for any of the coarse, dry grasses that had survived. As a consequence, our cattle wintered in good shape, thanks to the buried treasure we mined for them.

Tom House, temporarily suspended from his job as manager of a cotton gin at McAdoo, took on the feeding task, utilizing a power-driven box mounted on a truck to distribute the silage over the range. Tom never returned to his job at the gin, and was with us for seven years.

But the wheel of fortune had not ceased turning, and our situation continued to change.

20. The Grim Reaper Persists

Six years of drought came to an end in April, 1957. The initial showers were followed by slow, gentle rains. They eased the doubts we
had accumulated as previous hopes of relief had been stifled when
occasional thunderstorms were followed by more weeks of dry, dusty
weather. Results in our pastures were amazing. The areas of bare
soil that apparently harbored no potential of plant life proved to
be hiding grass seeds waiting for the right conditions, and soon even
the steep hillsides were turning green.

I had disposed of my cattle in 1955, selling the last of my cows
to Smith & Farris when they occupied the two big pastures of the
L7 Ranch adjoining us. The registered herd demanded my full attention, so I disposed of my livestock in order to concentrate all
my energies. Smith & Farris had bought the cattle and taken over
the lease the Whittaker Company obtained from Carl Craddock,
relieving the Californians of an expensive adventure that probably
dashed any illusions they held about the cattle business. Smith &
Farris also took up the lease on the SR Camp and the adjoining
pastures.

Rain and a new oil lease brought about improvement in our prospects. Although the Humble Oil Company paid a bonus of only
$5 an acre, it was a welcome advance over the $2 the Texas Company had paid ten years earlier. Humble performed systematic seis-
mic explorations during the next two years, then dropped the lease.

We built a house in Spur for our mother that she shared with
Randolph. The house was located next door to her good friend Mrs.
Link, a lot we obtained by buying and tearing down the old house
occupying it.

Following his crop failure in 1956, Jimmy moved to Navasota,
where his wife Eugenia took a teaching job, while Jimmy commuted
to Sam Houston University in Huntsville. Early in 1957 our mother,
making a tour of her South Texas relatives and friends, paid the
young couple a visit. While there, and in the daytime absence of
her hosts, she suffered a stroke and in falling, sustained severe fa-
cial cuts and abrasions. Neighbors discovered her wandering outside the house, bloody and incoherent, and summoned help.

When informed of her injury, Maude and I went immediately to

Navasota, finding her in the local hospital. Her speech was affected, but she was able to write legibly enough, although her vocabulary suffered confusion. We took her back to Spur by ambulance, where she recuperated under the care of Dr. Bob Alexander. She applied herself to the recovery of intelligible speech and in a matter of months overcame most of the disabilities brought on by the stroke.

Physical problems continued to harass the family, and in 1958 I underwent spinal surgery. I suppose exertions during the drought aggravated a malformation involving an extra lumbar vertebra, and I finally came to a point where I simply could not function. Various types of therapy produced no relief, and finally a Lubbock neurosurgeon repaired three ruptured discs. This got me back on my feet, but I was still hampered by continued disabilities and pain. It would be eight years before another neurosurgeon would perform orthopedic surgery to correct a previously overlooked condition.

A few months later our mother suffered a second stroke. Her condition did not improve, but did stabilize, leaving her in a condition requiring complete hospital care. Her throat and tongue were paralyzed, and she could neither speak nor swallow; nourishment came intravenously or through a tube. Additionally, she had lost all means of communication, unable to use her hands sufficiently for writing. We were fortunate in getting her admitted to the Baptist Geriatrics Hospital in San Angelo, where she could receive the specialized care necessary for survival.

In 1958 son George took over my farming operations. He had married in 1957 and, when jobs in South Texas and Crosbyton promised little future, readily accepted my proposal that he assume my agrarian activities, a function vacated when Graden Bass moved to a more promising situation near Spur.

Reese had expanded his seed business, taking in areas that included Arizona, Mexico, and Cuba, although the overthrow of the Batista regime terminated his plans to grow certified seeds there. In order to supervise this widely scattered enterprise, he traveled in his own plane, logging hundreds of hours annually. He was a skilful pilot in spite of an internal hemorrhage in 1937 that made his right eye useless. For most, this handicap would inhibit depth perception, but, like Wiley Post, he was an exception to the norm and had no difficulty in passing the licensing tests.

However, Reese had one failing typical of his general attitude: sometimes he took chances. Whether this played a part in a homeward flight from Arizona cannot be determined, for the evidence is clouded with contradictory indicators. But the salient fact remains: Reese was killed when he crashed in a dense fog near Lamesa, Dawson County, Texas, on December 31, 1959. He was accompanied by an employee, a young agronomist named Herbert Heimer. The plane caught fire when the impact ruptured the fuel tanks, and both bodies were badly burned. The Dawson County sheriff's office requested assistance in establishing identifications, and Reese's family asked me to take on that responsibility.

Alvie Ratheal, at that time sheriff of Crosby County, took me to Lamesa to view the bodies. We drove, at night, in the densest fog I can remember, and the intense gloom matched my feelings as we proceeded. I experienced apprehension bordering on panic as I considered the prospect confronting me. That anxiety relaxed when the Lamesa sheriff asked about the sizes of the two victims, and I told him that Heimer was seven inches taller than Reese. He said that was sufficient for identification, and I was spared the agony of viewing the charred remains of one with whom I had been so close.

Our mother was never informed of Reese's death. Persistent questions were raised in our minds when we visited her, and we wondered what doubts might have plagued her concerning her eldest son that she could not put into words, the more constant because of his protracted absence from her bedside.

Fannie McNeill died in July, 1960, after twenty months in the hospital and was buried at Spur alongside her husband and son. On two occasions the administrator of the San Angelo hospital had called us with a summons: "If you want to see your mother alive, you must get here within the next ten or twelve hours!" Each time, our two-hundred-mile dash found her wordlessly and successfully fighting for life. But the third attack was just too much for her.

Cattle prices improved as drought effects were overcome. A demand for restocking ranges depleted in the dry years assisted this. The situation indicated an expanding market for range bulls, and breeders regarded the future with optimism. However, a new and unexpected development created a miasma of doubt that retarded the Hereford cattle business for several years.

Dwarfism had made its appearance in many herds. A normal, healthy cow might produce a calf resembling a buffalo in shape: big in the shoulders, tapering to the hindquarters, with a short neck and short, knobby legs. Such calves did not grow off normally, and many died before reaching a stunted, gnomelike maturity. The causes of the abnormality were unknown to breeders, and its irregular occurrence augmented uncertainties. Commercial cattlemen grew wary in their purchases of bulls, a caution enhanced when many breeders concealed cases of dwarfism. Innuendo, falsifying, and sheer quackery added to the confusion and distrust.

One charlatan convinced Howard Hampton, Hereford breeder in New Mexico, that he could identify carriers of the dwarfism gene with a device he called a "profilometer." The inventor/operator claimed to detect potential producers of dwarf calves by measuring with his device the heads of mature cattle. Although Hampton's cows had produced no dwarfs, he had the man review his herd, and based on the examiner's report, sold a number of good cows for beef. Later, it was demonstrated that dwarfism did not exist in the Hampton cattle, and the destruction of some outstanding cows was a costly, needless fraud.

After a few years of turmoil, the American Hereford Association launched a campaign to straighten things out. Members were asked to report any Hereford matings that had produced dwarf calves, and the members responded well. Data analysis identified the tainted bloodlines, making reliable information available. To protect member breeders, this information was never published, but was made available on request. In a short time, dwarfism in purebred Herefords came under control.

As breeders, we all got a lesson in genetics. In the first place, we learned that dwarfism is a *recessive* characteristic, meaning that it can become manifest *only* if both parents are carriers of the dwarfism gene, and that *on the average,* this mating will produce a dwarf only one time out of four, and, *on the average* two calves would be carriers only, and one calf would be "clean." The probabilities possible in this contingency are so erratic that a dwarf could appear where none had occurred in its family tree in several preceding generations.

I had managed to build up our bull battery, including two important additions: Larry Domino 66, bought from O. H. McAllister of Rhome, Texas, in 1952 and in 1953, R Proud Mixer 607, bought from Tom Garrard of Tahoka. The Garrard bull proved to be a significant purchase, for when bred to our cows of strong Prince Domino Return ancestry, produced young bulls that commercial buyers desired.

Since dwarfism did not appear in our herd for some time, we escaped the early brunt of panic. Reason for the delay became apparent later on: our cow herd was clean, and until we raised a new generation of females sired by the bulls I had bought, we could expect no test of the bloodlines introduced by these purchases.

In 1956 we produced our first and only dwarf calf, and the Proud Mixer breeding stood condemned, for that bloodline was represented in both the sire and the dam of the calf. This brought about some drastic changes in our Hereford business. Determined to produce no more questionable registered cattle, we culled out all the cows sired by doubtful bulls, forming with them a commercial herd and retaining for registry only those cows whose pedigrees were limited to proven clean bloodlines.

The descendants of cattle bred by Gudgell & Simpson of Independence, Missouri, were recognized nationally as clean of dwarfism even before the Hereford association conducted its survey. This occurred because a breeders' association had preserved these cattle as a separate and exclusive bloodline by accepting as "straight bred" only those individuals whose ancestry was confined to cattle produced by Gudgell & Simpson, who had dispersed their herd in 1916. A bull named Anxiety 4th, imported from England, was the chief sire used by the Missouri partnership. The group preserving the bloodline was named the Anxiety 4th Hereford Breeders Association.

They conducted an annual consignment sale, varying the location. In 1956 the sale was held in Amarillo, and I bought a bull bred by Joe Ruther & Son of Butler, Oklahoma. Using this bull on our Prince Domino Return cows, we produced calves we could guarantee free from dwarfism. But heifers sired by the Ruther bull seldom came up to our standards of excellence, and we accumulated a group of Hereford cows of admirable ancestry, but rather ordinary appearance.

In 1961 I bought a bull bred by Alton and Arlan Youngblood in a consignment sale at Big Spring. It proved to be the best addition to our herd made at any time under my administration. In breeding livestock, sometimes a particular mating will produce progeny of uniformly good quality, sometimes exceeding the quality of the parents. Such an occurrence has been dubbed a "nick." The service of the Youngblood bull on cows sired by the Ruther bull qualified for such a label, and we were highly pleased with the results obtained by the combination.

Appointed, after the death of my father as the administrator of his estate, I operated the cattle business as a family partnership, while Reese and I farmed the cultivated land as tenants. I did not individually restock any of the pastures owned by M. E. Mitchell, nor that belonging to the L. J. McNeill family, subleasing the SR Camp and adjoining pastures to a succession of cattlemen that finally found in Stanton Brunson a continuous occupant.

In a division of the cattle and ranching equipment in 1964, George and I bought the two-thirds interest owned by our mother's other heirs, assuming the leasehold usage of lands belonging to Roland Jones, M. E. Mitchell, and the heirs of Jim and Jud McNeill. This brought George into an ownership role in the cattle business. However, he continued to live in Crosbyton, having bought our house there when we moved to Austin in 1962.

My health had not improved, and we sought Austin's educational advantages for our two daughters. Ann had acquired a little sister when Paula, named for her grandmother Pauline Clemmons, was born in 1951. That Maude's family (her mother and two sisters) was living in Austin made residence there especially pleasant. For three years I commuted to the ranch, establishing bachelor quarters in the ranch house vacated in 1952 when Mother and Randolph moved to Spur.

The first weeks of my solitary residency were not pleasant ones. The ranch house had been treated as a family storehouse, acquiring a wide variety of items for storage, isolation, and elimination. West Texas sandstorms had contributed plenty of dust, and mice and rats adopted the whole situation as ideal. I moved in about the middle of a hot summer and discovered, to my dismay, that the one window unit air conditioner was occupied by the ripened carcass of a snake that had managed an entrance but did not find an exit. I spent some unpleasant hours scrubbing, cleaning, and rearranging to restore a livable condition to just part of the house. By the summer

George D. McNeill on Rusty

of 1963 with Maude's assistance, the place was restored to its original condition, and with the two girls and their guest, we spent most of the summer there.

George increased our commercial herd, utilizing pastures that I had previously stocked with my own cattle, and reducing our registered cows to about a hundred head. Tom House looked after the cattle until 1964, living, by preference, in one of the houses at the farm.

By 1965 George had demonstrated his ability to manage our cattle business without my assistance and supervision, and I accepted an appointment with a federal agency as a field representative for the regional division of the Office of Economic Opportunity in Austin. I elected to work in rural areas, and by demonstrating a willingness to accept difficult travel assignments, wound up doing a considerable amount of it in West Texas.

This arrangement enabled me to spend occasional weekends at the ranch. George sold the Crosbyton house in 1966 and moved to the ranch after he and his brother-in-law, Frank Nelson Brixey, had made some extensive repairs and improvements to the house. Thereafter I found a warm welcome when my itinerary allowed me to spend a couple of days with him and his family. We no longer depended on consignment sales as an outlet for our bulls. Local demand was sufficient to absorb the reduced number raised. No registered heifers were offered for sale, as we selected the tops for maintaining the registered herd and retained the rest for building up the commercial cattle. The late 1960s were busy times for George, for he took on the job of looking after the cattle single-handed, while attending to the farming with the help of one tractor driver. Tom House had qualified for Social Security and moved to Fisher County, the area of his origin.

One development made George's setup feasible. The government's success in controlling the screwworm curse did away with having to watch over the cattle closely during warm months. But this blessing did not remove the need for frequent surveys of the pastures and checking on fences, windmills, other watering places, and strays (particularly alien bulls), plus the many potential and unfortunate situations that can occur among cattle on the range.

Pressed for time, George introduced his own expedient method of checking on conditions, an innovation that the horses should have appreciated. He simply loaded a few sacks of the range pellets the cattle were accustomed to and called them together by honking the horn in his pickup, a sound they recognized as an invitation to dine. Then after he had distributed enough feed to make a meaningful assembly, he would count and inspect to see if all were present and in good condition.

The Bridwell Ranch, located up Blanco Canyon on land formerly owned by Sidney Webb, had acquired a new foreman in Bobby Adams. He manifested a neighborliness not characteristic of previous personnel on the outfit. This helped establish a connection that developed in succeeding years, involving additional employees and facilities. Clifford Tinsley, general manager of the Bridwell ranches, regarded all this with benign approval.

A similar neighborly relationship developed with the ranch Dr.

"Canyon Gang" at work

O. W. English owned under the management of his son, Otis. Since then the "Canyon Gang" has cooperated in working cattle, and in spite of some changes in faces, does so with a maximum of good fellowship and efficiency.

21. Freezes and Fractures

Mark Twain wrote a short novel, *The American Claimant,* in which the absence of any reference to weather is not noticeable if the reader follows a common practice of skipping the author's own comment. I doubt that any such exclusion would go unheeded in a ranch history covering a significant time period. In such a story, climatic conditions play too important a part to be ignored.

The trials and discomforts of cowpunchers living under chuck wagon circumstances have been related at length, with special attention to cold and wintry seasons. In years past inadequate clothing worsened their plight, a situation resulting from both lack of personal funds and slow development of appropriate apparel.

An effective garment often carried in my earlier years was a slicker — the cowboy's raincoat. Branded "Alligator," it was a bright yellow and made by some manufacturer whose name I do not remember. It was described as the "pommel" type, with a vent cut high in the back to allow the coat to drape over either side of the horse, covering the rider's legs and feet. It was roomy enough to cover much of the saddle.

The chief virtue of a slicker in cold weather was its effectiveness as a windbreak. Its major drawback was its unhandy size and bulk, causing an owner to recall the cowboy's lament: "Thunderin' and lightnin' and comin' on to rain, And my damned old slicker's in the wagon again!"

My life as cowpuncher never called for me to be exposed to the elements in a twenty-four-hour cycle, and most exposures occurred during daytime. But some of those days were quite chilly. I recall a morning in 1920 when our horses' tails froze stiff from wind-whipped water splashed on them as we crossed White River on our way to the West Pasture. Before sending me up the Cap Rock, my father inquired about my comfort, and when I told him my feet were cold, he dismounted under the protection of a low bluff, pulled off his boots, and donated one of the three pairs of socks he was wearing.

At that early age I was proud to be assigned the job of leading the drive, loping around the outer edge of the pastures to start cattle toward the center. In the fall of 1921 we set out to gather the cattle in the East Pasture, and I went north along the east fence to start any cattle toward the "breaks" that I found on the plains, shoving them off the Cap Rock to join the rest of the drive. It was a bright, crisp November morning, cool but not cold, without a cloud in the sky.

My ride took me three miles to the northeast corner of the pasture. By the time I reached that point the wind had shifted to the north and a few clouds had appeared. Nowhere in that level expanse could I see any cattle, and their ability to anticipate the weather soon became apparent. They had gone to shelter in the rough country below. By the time I reached the Cap Rock at the west end of my tour, the wind had increased, clouds covered the sky, and a cold mist was falling.

A mile to the south I could see a cluster of cattle and recognized Guy Merriman herding them. More cattle were directly below me, and I picked them up when I made the descent. However, they ran south with the wind, and I had to make a run to turn them west toward the roundup ground at China Hollow. Although I put together a sizable bunch, my attempts to move them cross-wind westward were unsuccessful. The wind was still rising, and the mist was forming icy crusts on bushes and rocks.

I rode up on a knoll to check on Guy, and although I could not hear him holler, I could see that he was busy, striving, as I was, to move cattle west. Assuming from his actions that the drive was still operating, I went back to my own frustrating situation.

It had not improved during my absence. The cattle were not inclined to run off, but try as I might, I could not make them go west. Twice more I went to check on Guy, depending on his actions as the indicator of my father's decision to continue the roundup, but finally decided that a conference was in order and loped down to discuss the problem. I told Guy of my assumption that the drive was continuing, based on his actions. We had a cold laugh when it became apparent that he had been checking on me when I was not looking his way, and my activities had convinced him that the work was still in progress.

Agreeing that the situation was hopeless, we set out to find the rest of the crew, including Tom McKnight, who was at that time living at the SR Camp, plus two hands whose names I do not recall. We found the two nameless ones, but failed to find Tom or my father. Assuming that they had already quit the drive, we rode across White River to the camp, where Tom's wife was expecting us for the noon meal.

The missing pair was not there. Finally, after Mrs. McKnight had filled us with coffee and hot food, Tom came in, his face blue with the cold.

About the middle of the afternoon the cold mist ceased and we decided to look for my father. While saddling our horses, he rode up, dry and apparently none the worse for the weather. When we inquired about his absence, he replied, with a chuckle, "I've got sense enough to come in out of the rain!"

He had taken refuge under an overhanging ledge on Waddell Draw, built a fire, and waited for the weather to improve.

I remembered this episode forty-seven years later, when another sudden change in the weather forced us to call off a roundup in the same area. I had arranged to help brand and identify registered calves in the Waddell Pasture; John Ancell, Stanton Brunson's current ranch hand, plus Kenneth Sellers, Marvin Heinrich, and R. L. Martin assisted us.

A pleasant morning was spoiled when a cold, wet norther made us aware that we were not properly dressed. Determined to get the job done while I was available, George continued working the herd until he noticed that John Ancell was wrapping his rope around his body. When George investigated, he found that the cowboy was trying to add another layer of fiber over the light jacket he was wearing, a recourse John was quick to defend.

"George," he said, "I have never been so cold in my life. I've about made up my mind to ride to my pickup, load this horse and go home. If Mr. Brunson fires me, it will beat freezing to death here!"

He made his point, and George soon had my approval for calling off the work, for I too welcomed an opportunity to escape an extremely uncomfortable situation.

By the time we got to the ranch house the cold drizzle was succeeded by wind-blown snowflakes. After a hasty meal, I got in my car and headed for Austin, succeeding in getting ahead of a heavy snowfall that was just beginning. The blizzard continued through most of the night, depositing fourteen inches of snow underlaid with two inches of ice.

We had cattle grazing wheat fields at the farm. Realizing their plight, George made preparations the next morning to go to their relief. For the trip he chose a young horse called Chester, likening his attitude and conduct to Marshall Dillon's deputy in the television series "Gunsmoke" — willing but not very wise. Before starting, George pulled the horse's shoes off to eliminate the formation of "stilts," caused when snow packs within the confines of the iron shoes and builds into unstable mounds.

Arrived at the west field, he found the cattle gathered in mesquite trees and bushes just inside the fence. The drifting snow had formed what he called "igloos" in the brush, each with its bovine occupants. When he cut the fence, the cattle fairly exploded from their impromptu shelters and headed for the Cap Rock in a trot. He found a similar situation in the east field, except that not all the cows could take advantage of their release. Some of them had taken refuge in a shallow valley just above the Cap Rock, and eighteen of them were dead.

For our area, this was probably the worst blizzard since 1918, but there was a far greater accumulation of snow that covered most of the grass and stayed on the ground for over two weeks. Fortunately, George had put up a quantity of baled hay, and with the assistance of a farmhand, fed the cattle in small pastures near the farm.

We did not lose any more cows and ascribed the death losses to grass tetany, a magnesium deficiency commonly referred to as wheat poison that, combined with the severe weather, proved fatal in this instance.

In November, 1971, Randolph Calvin McNeill died, victim of a combination of ailments that included diabetes and emphysema. Ran never married and lived with our mother until illness removed her from the house we built for them in Spur. His interest in two-way radio, cultivated at the Spur police station, won him a job as night dispatcher in the sheriff's office at Crosbyton, a function he enjoyed and performed for several years.

His final illness was not painful, and I was sitting by his bedside when he drew his last breath. He was buried in the cemetery at Spur, joining there his parents and his brother Reese in the family burial plot.

Under George's management and diligence, things progressed well at the ranch through the late 1960s and early 1970s, punctuated by the usual ups and downs that lend variety to agricultural production. When the regional office of OEO moved to Dallas in 1970, I was drawn closer in proximity to the ranch, but found fewer opportunities to take part in activities there as my duties and areas of responsibility expanded.

George proposed that we take back the SR Camp and the adjacent pastures that we had been leasing to Stanton Brunson, which we did as of January 1, 1972. Soon thereafter George began looking for cows for restocking that acreage, no easy task at the time, for stocker cows were in strong demand. This expansion of our comparatively small cattle-raising venture soon proved to George that his solitary caretaking activities, innovative though they may have been, were increasingly burdensome for one who was also cultivating sixteen hundred acres of farmland. He began, tactfully, advancing the idea that my permanent presence at the ranch would be welcomed.

His problems intensified when he was injured while helping work cattle on the neighboring Bridwell Ranch. He was thrown from his horse and suffered a smashed collarbone, a couple of broken ribs, and a thumb broken and disjointed when he attempted to maintain his hold on the bridle reins. The clavicle was too thoroughly crushed for repair by standard procedures. Somehow Dr. Dale Rhodes herded the bits and pieces into a continuous assemblage, and managed to immobilize the area until the mass of fragments knitted together.

Jim McNeill used to say that anyone extensively involved with horses usually had some disfigurement to show for it: George's is a collar bone several times the usual size, and mine a permanent detour in the spinal column.

Naturally, the period of immobility brought on by the accident changed George's schedule from a burden to a predicament, and his requests for my return became all the more urgent. I submitted my resignation to OEO, effective October 1. To my delight, Maude expressed a desire to live on the ranch, selecting a spot just under the Cap Rock with a view that took in a panorama of ranch country extending forty miles to the butte south of Post known as Flat Top. We arranged for the construction of a house with a firm in Lubbock that built it on their lot, then moved it, complete, to the ranch. Construction was started in April, and we moved in just before Christmas, 1973.

Convinced of the need for a hand to help with the cattle, in 1972 George had bought a five-room house, previously the farm home of Dennis and Rachel Taylor, and had it moved to a location just above the Cap Rock. We acquired a cowhand in Ronnie McCravey; his competence in welding and carpentry fitted him for our needs, as did his experience with cattle and horses, a combination of skills desirable on modern small ranches.

We added a barn and corrals to the place that George had dubbed C Camp, honoring the brand by which Jim McNeill identified his registered Herefords. We now had camps honoring brands established by the previous two generations of McNeills.

C Camp

Our celebration of Christmas marked 1973 as a satisfying year, for crops were good, cattle prices higher, George had recovered from his accident, we were in a new house on the land of our heritage, and the future looked bright.

But dry weather in the spring of 1974 set the stage for changes. A pleasant Sunday afternoon was spoiled when George telephoned to tell me that the ranch house was on fire. I jumped in a pickup and hastened to the scene. The fire had broken out on the second floor; smoke poured from the upper windows, and it looked as if the old house was doomed. The volunteer fire company at Spur had been called and was on its way, but time for the twenty-one-mile trip seemed to offer little hope before the blaze might break through the roof and become uncontrollable.

It was imperative to get some water to the fire in hopes of retarding its progress, but attempts to take a hose up the stairs were frus-

J. C. ("Cap") McNeill III, 1973

trated by smoke so dense no one could even crawl to the second floor. Circumstances produced a hero in the person of Kent Sellers, Barbara's teenaged nephew. An iron pipe supporting a television aerial had been erected close to the windows on the west side of the house, and the boy shinnied up that slender shaft, pulled a hose through a window, and squirted some water on the blaze. It was enough to prevent the fire from penetrating the ceiling. When the firemen arrived, a deluge of water quenched the fire completely.

Smoke and water damage was extensive, upstairs and down, although the basic structure was unharmed. Reconstruction thereafter was a long, drawn-out process; a contractor selected by the insurance adjuster delayed progress and attempted to take advantage of the situation with inferior materials and inept workmanship. George's strenuous objections prevailed, and the contractor was dismissed. A second workman was selected, who tore out the crude efforts of his predecessor and restored the house to a condition that actually surpassed its former state. But many weeks of irritation, frustration, inconvenience, and discomfort were consumed in the restoration process.

Coupled with other untoward developments, the cattle market suffered a typical slump. The strong demand for stocker cows in 1972 and 1973 should have been a warning, and our expansion was typical of the means by which overpopulation results in lower prices. Consequently, the fair cost of the cows we bought in 1973 was a hundred dollars too high in 1974.

Rainfall was below normal throughout the year, but sufficient for planting crops. Unfortunately, a rain that fell in June was accompanied by wind and lots of hail. The damage was severe. Growing crops were destroyed, and of the young trees I had planted around the house only one survived. Storm windows were broken, buildings at the farm sustained damages indicating tornadic winds, and a large corrugated iron granary was destroyed. Because of the dry spring and poor prospects for a harvest, we had turned cattle in on the wheat, thereby unwittingly salvaging the grazing out of a crop that would have been a total loss had we let it go on toward maturity.

One act of kindness stands out in the year's misfortunes. Frank Sellers, Barbara's father, brought his three sons and their tractors to help replant cotton, thereby saving us valuable time. The entire crop was replanted in two days, and the fact that we harvested an

average crop that fall must be credited, at least in part, to this un-
solicited deed of friendship.

Although the spinal malformation that put me in the hospital
in 1958 was not passed on as a family trait, by 1975 George too was
prostrated with an ailing back. Lubbock doctors found the damage
to herniated discs too severe for repair and resorted to fusing the
implicated vertebrae together. The operation was successful, but convalescence slow, and his activities very limited for several weeks.

A couple of years previous to this he had hired Joe Lee Childers
for farm work, a loyal black man whose tenure on the place has
extended over many years. Inconveniently, George's hospitalization
occurred just before planting time, but with me as messenger con-
veying instructions to Joe and making the necessary trips for supplies and repairs, the crop was planted in good shape. Ronnie Mc-
Cravey, meanwhile, looked after the cattle.

When George was able to get up and move around in the house,
his doctor advised short walks outdoors.

"For example," said Dr. Jack Dunn, "start by walking out to the
mailbox." Perceiving some doubt on George's part, he asked, "By
the way, how far is it to your mailbox?"

"Five miles," answered George, with a grin.

"Forget it!" said the doctor, with emphasis.

But walking became a large part of George's daily regimen, a process to which he devoted himself, striving to regain the mobility his
vocation required. After several weeks of recuperation, he resumed
parts of his routine.

In conformity, my back problems, never eliminated fully by surgery, became increasingly troublesome, and I was frequently put out
of action for days at a time. But the same Dr. Dunn located an area
of constricted nerves below the site of the operation I had in 1958
and, in his own words, "hacked out a proper channel for some
pinched nerves." Significant relief resulted, although years of ne-
glect left me with limits in the use of my left leg, causing me some
difficulty in mounting a horse.

In October, 1977, Mary Emily Mitchell, known as M. E. to family and friends, died after several years in a Brazoria County nursing home to which she had consigned herself when she felt that se-

nility might cause her to be a burden to the family. The last survivor of the Captain's children, she was a little over one hundred years old.

Childless, her maternal inclinations showed early in her attentions to her younger sisters after the untimely death of their mother in 1890. It was continued in her solicitude toward her nieces and nephews, particularly those of her brothers, Jim and Jud, for whom she cherished an unfaltering admiration.

At the time of her death, her estate consisted principally of the six sections deeded her by the Captain in 1930. Not many years thereafter she had deeded the land to her brothers' children, retaining a life estate in the property to ensure herself some income until her death.

22. Closing the Century

Definite changes have occurred in the types of cattle that have worn the SR brand in Blanco Canyon since the Captain drove fifteen hundred head to the COE Spring on White River in 1883. His were of the nondescript kind prevalent on most Texas ranges at the time. It was a type that seemed to prevail along the Gulf Coast longer than elsewhere. It can hardly be classified as Longhorn, for few of them possessed the essential characteristic by which that "breed" is identified. As a matter of fact, designating these cattle as a type is probably incorrect. The wide deviations among them are their most notable attribute, a specialty that enabled George Williamson, in an 1890 letter to the Captain, to identify one particular cow out of two thousand by describing her distinctive markings.

Traces of this diversity were still apparent by the time I came along, and the continued use of Hereford bulls had not completely eliminated some mottled faces and unique markings from the Side R cows held in the West Pasture. I recall two steers included in the herd sold to Lee Bivins in 1917; these steers were five years old, having escaped roundups in previous years. They had horns that were, in a comparative sense, impressive, although I doubt that they would qualify in the estimation of a present-day Longhorn fancier.

I suspect my recollection is not based so much on the steers' appearance as it is on having them pointed out to me by Floyd Wilhoit with his assurance, while fondling his rope, that they would not get away again. But I do recall that, in appearance, they did not possess the typical markings of white-faced Herefords.

In time, the continued use of good Hereford bulls eliminated distinctions that had existed between the Side R descendants of the Captain's original herd and the Hip R descendants of the Boles heifers. By the time the cattle were divided among the heirs in 1930 the ranch was stocked with a herd of excellent Hereford cows, and the remnant of nine-year-old cows I bought from my aunt in 1942 would have compared favorably with most anyone's commercial Herefords.

The Hereford breed has dominated Western ranges for most of my years of observation. It is noted for its prolificacy, hardiness, and the quality of the beef produced. But during that time variations in type have been developed through selective breeding, some of which have, in the long run, deterred rather than advanced the superiority of the breed.

Such a deviation occurred during a period of two decades or more, with corrective trends developing in or around the 1960s. The fallacy seems to have had its origin in "club" shows, that is, the programs involving youngsters who feed, groom, and exhibit beef calves for prizes and proceeds obtained in subsidized auction sales.

I am in no position to ascribe this development to the club calf programs alone, for a look at the illustrations in old Hereford sales catalogs finds pictures of noted sires as drawn by commercial artists, depicting bulls with smooth, rectangular bodies, extremely deep and supported on very short legs. These idealized illustrations may have influenced contest judges and breeders in the assumption that such a conformation was that toward which they should aspire.

At any rate, we breeders of registered Herefords were subjected to influences in the stock shows and sales rings to try for what was frequently referred to as the club type. The same proponents also recommended cattle of smaller size, based on the assumption that they reached maturity earlier and would thereby produce prime beef more quickly in the feedlots.

Range men did not find this trend fully acceptable. Their ideas were represented by cattle frequently (and sometimes patronizingly) referred to as the "cowman's type." Their objections won support in agricultural colleges, where research demonstrated faults in the club types, and publicized the facts with pictures of steers before and after the hides had been removed. These showed that the carcasses of the smooth, blocky, short-legged cattle bore masses of fat that filled out their hides with tallow for which neither the housewife nor the restaurateur had any use. It served only to fill out some parts of the animals body where muscular tissue did not exist, lending the animal a smooth outward appearance.

As a result of this scientific approach, we now have Hereford sires more acceptable to range men that possess, in the language of the sales rings, "elevation" (height) and "stretch" (body length), with emphasis on increased size with special attention to areas that provide desirable cuts of beef. A remaining sphere of investigation might study the effects of size and conformation on efficiency in converting grass and concentrates into lean meat.

We still maintain a small registered Hereford herd of a hundred cows, purchasing bulls that conform to present standards in type and size, but we have strayed away from the strict Hereford bloodlines in the production of commercial calves. Our change in policy resulted from our own experiences, which were initiated for reasons other than developing a better type of beef animal.

For years it had been our practice to breed most of our cows to calve in the fall, a deviation from former times and natural bovine inclinations. Under free, uncontrolled circumstances, cattle tend to breed in the summer and calve in the spring. But with supplemental feeding, the fall calves do better and weigh more at weaning time.

Calving problems with heifers caused us to seek crossbreeding that would produce smaller calves at birth. We tried using Jersey bulls, as did many other cow/calf operators. This cross eliminated practically all our calving difficulties, but produced calves whose conformation and growth included too many dairy characteristics to sell well for beef purposes.

Following the advice of Paul Newman, cattle dealer at Lubbock, we started using Angus bulls with our heifers in the 1960s. For this purpose Paul bought for us Angus bulls he had found effective in producing the desired results, violating the standards by which "good" bulls might be evaluated. He looked for small, light-boned bulls with narrow hips and shoulders, and with small heads.

We were agreeably surprised to find that the calves sired by these inferior black bulls not only reduced the heifers' calving problems, but grew off well and were accepted by most buyers at a price level comparable to Hereford calves. The experience introduced us to the value of crossbreeding, and we began using good Angus bulls with some of our Hereford cows, finding therein that additional vigor resulted from selective crossing of different branches of the bovine species. The Angus characteristics showed in the black bodies of these calves, the Hereford in their white faces, and "black baldies" became the descriptive term by which this popular type was identified.

The first extensive crossbreeding practice I observed involving breeds originating outside the British Isles included Brahmans, or Zebus, regarded as sacred in India, their country of origin. However, as the practice caught on, several European breeds have been introduced — Charolais, Simmental, Limousin, and Chianina, and others. Most of these originated in France, and their muscular development can often be ascribed to selective breeding for draft purposes.

Seeking further carcass improvement aimed at producing choice cuts, lean meat, and less waste, we started using some Limousin bulls about 1974, and have continued the practice with satisfactory results. This cross is not appropriate for breeding heifers, and we switched to Longhorn bulls for that service. This has been successful so far as the calving process is concerned, but has not produced calves of the quality desired. A cross involving Angus and Brahman bloodlines, called Brangus, is a probable answer to this situation.

Indeed, all this presents a marked change from the days when a group of multicolored calves would be labelled mixed breed and summarily characterized as inferior. Present standards go beyond color, markings, and strict uniformity in breed characteristics to look beneath the hide and appraise the potential for prime beef.

Since our fall calves are now weaned in the late summer, sales that used to take place in the late fall have been moved up to about the first of August. As comparatively small operators, we did not attract much attention from dealers accustomed to buying calves from the big ranches. However, George established contacts with reliable buyers whose offers were in line with current markets. They could be depended on to carry out verbal agreements and, usually, without a deposit of earnest money guaranteeing fulfillment of the trade.

191

Sometimes deliveries were delayed as our contacts explored their outlets for placing the calves we were offering. So, recalling the times when SR calves were often contracted in the spring or early summer for delivery about the first of November, I suggested that we try for earlier deals wherein the delivery date could be established well in advance, eliminating the uncertainties in our schedule of operations.

George's telephoned presentations did not arouse much enthusiasm among the buyers with whom we had previously dealt, but he finally made a deal with Dalby Fleming of Amarillo, who had, in recent years, been our most consistent purchaser and knew the quality and characteristics of our cattle. The price agreed on was 65 cents a pound for steer calves, 60 cents for heifers, a figure in line with the prevailing market on choice, heavy calves.

My idea cost us money, for by the time delivery date arrived, the cattle market had made spectacular advances, and our calves were worth much more than the contract price. That advance was reflected in our 1979 sales, when the same buyer paid us $1 a pound for steer calves and 90 cents for heifers. The deal was made by CB radio. This was the highest price we have ever achieved for commercial calves, before or since, and public reaction severely curtailed retail beef sales. By 1981 the price of comparable calves had dropped by 30 percent. Unfortunately, the averages have not improved materially since, although the increases in production costs have continued their steady advance.

Our production of Hereford bulls has been limited in recent years, and the small herd of a hundred cows has been maintained principally to provide a foundation of good females. Our most consistent outlet for Hereford bulls has been in the Big Bend area, where the hardiness and prolificacy of Herefords is still respected in that rugged and semiarid section. Two buyers there have taken most of our production, seldom coming to see the cattle, and usually taking whatever we have on hand. A variation to this emerged when one buyer requested crossbred bull calves—half-Hereford and half-Limousin—and is repeating with an order for several more.

In 1982, we celebrated one hundred years of the family's continuous agricultural operation on the same land bought by Captain McNeill. The Texas Department of Agriculture conducts a program

Cap McNeill on Goober, 1984

recognizing families who have achieved this distinction, with a ceremony conducted in the rotunda of the state capitol in Austin. On November 10, 1982, George, Jimmy, and I represented the family on this occasion. Commissioner of Agriculture Reagan Brown presented us a scroll, after which the three of us were guests at a reception in the commissioner's offices.

A short resumé of the ranch's history is included in a booklet the state published and distributed among the several recipients qualified in that particular year. We were also certified for the casting of a plaque identifying the ranch, with a short account of its founding and the family members involved through the years. This plaque is posted in front of our house on Section 2 of Block 28, one of those included in the original purchase from the New York & Texas Land Company. A similar historical plaque was approved for the ranch house, honoring its builder, Handy Cole, and subsequent owners, J. C. McNeill, Jr., and Roland Jones.

We dedicated these plaques with a barbecue at the ranch house August 7, 1982, with over four hundred invited guests present, including a large number of the Captain's descendants. Although most of the family members on hand came from South Texas, we also had kindred and friends from New York, Illinois, California, and points in between.

Our guests sat on hay bales scattered about in the ranch house yard, and ate a traditional barbecue meal catered by a Lubbock service. The front porch served as a speaker's rostrum for a short program of greetings, followed by a dedicatory address by Harold "Bo" Brown, representing the Ranching Heritage Association of Lubbock and Texas Tech University.

Afterward, a wholehearted visiting session occupied most of those in attendance, with dancing in the four-car garage continuing into the night.

A map of Texas showing all the counties where families have continuously occupied and operated farms and ranches for a full century, up to and including those succeeding in 1982, shows Crosby County isolated from others. The nearest is Jones County, southeast by over a hundred miles. Recognition accorded there was in deference to S. M. Swenson's first purchase of a West Texas ranch, also in 1882. Naturally, the areas previously qualified are in por-

Present SR ranch headquarters

tions of the state where settlement occurred earlier, evidence that the Captain was among the first who foresaw the importance of owning land in the Blanco Canyon.

Survival and optimism tend to mitigate the pain and anguish of the past, shifting emphasis to recollections of circumstances, personages, and events that were pleasant. This inclination, assumed present in most individuals, made this review of the SR Ranch, its environs, and the people connected with its operations, a gratifying experience for me. I suspect there will be a few readers whose bygone connections with the place and its personnel may let them experience an echo of my feelings and expand the story with their own recollections.

By any standards, Blanco Canyon is not a repetition of the Garden of Eden, however treasured by many, a conclusion at which the reader may already have arrived. Variously, it is a land of charm

195

and brutality, generosity and denial; lovely after a May shower, cruel in a March sandstorm or a January blizzard; a land of marginal rainfall where weather conditions create high hopes that sometimes evaporate in drought and caused a longtime resident to say to his mate: "Wife, we've spent most of our forty years here just waiting for a rain!"

But, significantly, they located here by preference, and it seems safe to assume that the same motivation made them stay. The McNeills are apparently a further instance of the same attachment.

Index

The McNeill's SR Ranch was composed into type on a Compugraphic digital phototypesetter in eleven point Times Roman with two points of spacing between the lines. Times Roman was also selected for display. The book was designed by Jim Billingsley, composed into type by Metricomp, Inc., printed offset by Thomson-Shore, Inc., and bound by John H. Dekker & Sons. The paper on which this book is printed is designed for an effective life of at least three hundred years.

TEXAS A&M UNIVERSITY PRESS : COLLEGE STATION